Cambridge Elements ☰

Elements in Philosophy of Mind
edited by
Keith Frankish
The University of Sheffield

ANIMAL MINDS

Marta Halina
University of Cambridge

CAMBRIDGE
UNIVERSITY PRESS

Shaftesbury Road, Cambridge CB2 8EA, United Kingdom

One Liberty Plaza, 20th Floor, New York, NY 10006, USA

477 Williamstown Road, Port Melbourne, VIC 3207, Australia

314–321, 3rd Floor, Plot 3, Splendor Forum, Jasola District Centre, New Delhi – 110025, India

103 Penang Road, #05–06/07, Visioncrest Commercial, Singapore 238467

Cambridge University Press is part of Cambridge University Press & Assessment, a department of the University of Cambridge.

We share the University's mission to contribute to society through the pursuit of education, learning and research at the highest international levels of excellence.

www.cambridge.org
Information on this title: www.cambridge.org/9781009517867

DOI: 10.1017/9781009119962

When citing this work, please include a reference to the DOI 10.1017/9781009119962

First published 2024

A catalogue record for this publication is available from the British Library.

ISBN 978-1-009-51786-7 Hardback
ISBN 978-1-009-11346-5 Paperback
ISSN 2633-9080 (online)
ISSN 2633-9072 (print)

Cambridge University Press & Assessment has no responsibility for the persistence or accuracy of URLs for external or third-party internet websites referred to in this publication and does not guarantee that any content on such websites is, or will remain, accurate or appropriate.

Animal Minds

Elements in Philosophy of Mind

DOI: 10.1017/9781009119962
First published online: February 2024

Marta Halina
University of Cambridge
Author for correspondence: Marta Halina, mh801@cam.ac.uk

Abstract: Animal minds are complex and diverse, making them difficult to study. This Element focuses on a question that has received much attention in the field of comparative cognition: "Do animals reason about unobservable variables like force and mental states?" The Element shows how researchers design studies and gather evidence to address this question. Despite the many virtues of current methods, hypotheses in comparative cognition are often underdetermined by the empirical evidence. Given this, philosophers and scientists have recently called for additional behavioral constraints on theorizing in the field. The Element endorses this proposal (known as "signature testing"), while also arguing that studies on animal minds would benefit from drawing more heavily on neuroscience and biology.

This Element also has a video abstract: www.Cambridge.org/EPMI_Halina

Keywords: nonhuman animal, cognition, evolution, causal reasoning, mindreading

ISBNs: 9781009517867 (HB), 9781009113465 (PB), 9781009119962 (OC)
ISSNs: 2633-9080 (online), 2633-9072 (print)

Contents

Introduction

Nonhuman animals (hereafter animals) engage in sophisticated behaviors. New Caledonian crows construct novel compound tools (von Bayern et al. 2018), western scrub jays remember not only which food items they've cached but also where and when they've cached them (Clayton et al. 2001), honey bees behave as if they have a concept of zero (Howard et al. 2018), and chimpanzees outperform human children on a variety of physical cognition tasks (Herrmann et al. 2007). Many animals also have complex nervous systems. Humans and chimpanzees diverged around 7 million years ago and have many brain structures in common. Even structures previously thought to be uniquely human, like areas of the paracingulate sulcus (linked to personality traits), have recently been found to be homologous across humans and chimpanzees (Amiez et al. 2021).[1] Mammals and birds diverged around 300 million years ago and thus differ more substantially in their neural structure. For example, it was not until after this divergence that the six-layered neocortex characteristic of mammalian brains evolved. Birds lack a neocortex, but have a nidopallium caudolaterale (NCL), which neuroscientists believe is functionally analogous to the mammalian neocortex. The NCL is larger in crows than other songbirds and appears to underpin many behavioral decisions, including those based on abstract principles (Veit & Nieder 2013).

Comparative psychologists and neuroscientists have learned a lot about the cognitive and behavioral abilities of animals over the last century. However, many questions remain unanswered. One outstanding question that has received a lot of attention from researchers is whether and how animals reason about so-called "unobservable" variables. Imagine, for example, seeing a crow approach a container of water. Floating on the water's surface is a grub – a rewarding food item for crows. The container is only half filled with water, though, so when the crow tries to extract the grub with its beak, it can't reach. Rather than giving up, however, the crow locates a small rock nearby, picks it up, and drops it into the container. This rock raises the water level so the grub is closer to the container's opening, but it's still not within reach. The crow, however, continues to drop rocks into the container until the grub is within reach. This problem is known as the Aesop's Fable task and has been used to investigate causal reasoning in rooks, crows, humans, and other animals (see Cheke et al. 2012; Jelbert et al. 2015).

Does the crow understand that heavy rocks are capable of displacing water? Do nonhuman animals more generally reason about unobservable causes like weight

---

[1] In this context, a feature is homologous or conserved when it has a similar structure or function across two or more taxa due to it being inherited by a common ancestor (see Halina & Bechtel 2013).

and force? If so, does this mean that they can reason about other unobservable variables like the beliefs and desires of another agent? Comparative cognition researchers have conducted numerous carefully controlled experiments with the aim of addressing these questions, but there is still major disagreement in the field regarding the answers. In this Element, I will examine this debate over whether animals reason about unobservable variables. This debate is important in part because it's a striking example of researchers providing different answers to Darwin's question regarding whether humans and other species should be understood as mentally different in degree or in kind. Darwin writes:

> If no organic being excepting man had possessed any mental power, or if his powers had been of a wholly different nature from those of the lower animals, then we should never have been able to convince ourselves that our high faculties had been gradually developed. But it can be shewn that there is no fundamental difference of this kind. (Darwin 1875, p. 65)

Although Darwinian evolution is widely accepted among comparative cognition researchers, there remains disagreement over how psychologically similar humans are to other animals. In the case of reasoning about unobservable variables, many researchers view human and nonhuman animals as differing in degree (Call & Tomasello 2008; Krupenye & Call 2019). Others, however, think this capacity represents a fundamental split between humans and all other animals. For example, Penn et al. (2008) argue that "Darwin was mistaken" and that there is a "profound discontinuity between human and animal minds" in this regard (p. 109). According to Penn and colleagues, only humans reason about unobservable variables and this makes them radically different from all other animals.

This debate also provides an entry point into important questions regarding how to study animal minds (Andrews 2020; Halina 2023). Researchers working in comparative cognition seek "not just to confirm that animals are (or are not) capable of doing something 'clever' but to discover *how* they do what they do" (Shettleworth 2012, p. 4). Crows drop nuts onto roads and retrieve the cracked nuts (Shettleworth 2010). Do they do this because they've learned that cars are useful nut-cracking tools or because they've evolved to crack shells by dropping them from a height (with no awareness of the effects of cars on nuts)? In order to choose amongst competing explanations, comparative cognition researchers conduct experiments designed to rule out plausible alternative hypotheses. As we will see, disagreements about whether animals reason about unobservable variables are due in large part to disagreements about whether there is enough direct and indirect evidence to support this claim. Investigating this debate will give us insight into what is needed to draw inferences about animal minds.

This Element proceeds as follows. I begin in Section 1 by introducing the diverse research aims of comparative cognition. It is important to keep these aims in mind, as different aims require different methods for success. Drawing on philosophy of science, I also introduce a general framework for thinking about the relationship between theory and evidence, which will help guide us in evaluating claims about animal minds. In Section 2, I introduce how researchers empirically investigate animal minds, focusing on those methods aimed at determining whether animals reason about unobservable variables. Here I examine the target hypotheses researchers aim to test, as well as the alternative accounts they attempt to eliminate. In Section 3, I consider two major challenges to the methods used in this research program. First, some researchers argue that the mainstream approaches used to investigate whether animals reason about unobservable variables are deeply misguided and should be replaced by an alternative approach. I argue that this concern is ultimately unpersuasive. However, a second challenge is that both mainstream and alternative approaches are plagued by problems of underdetermination. This latter challenge, I argue, prevents researchers from establishing strong warrant for the hypothesis that animals reason about unobservable variables. In Section 4, I consider two promising approaches to resolving these problems of underdetermination: signature testing and mechanistic constraints. Comparative cognition researchers currently rely almost exclusively on the results of pass/fail behavioral tasks for evaluating cognitive hypotheses. The behavior, brains, and bodies of animals, however, are complex and diverse. Additional constraints are needed to identify the mechanisms responsible for a given behavioral phenomenon. I draw on research in philosophy of science, as well as other scientific fields (e.g., biology and chemistry), to show how additional information-processing and mechanistic constraints can improve hypothesis evaluation when investigating animal minds.

1 Comparative Cognition

Before introducing the details involved in investigating animals' abilities to reason about unobservable variables, it is important to step back and consider two issues that will help frame our discussion. First, comparative cognition is a vast field with a multitude of aims. Clarifying the aims that concern us in this Element will help us focus our discussion (Section 1.1). Second, one of the central goals of this Element is to evaluate what we know about animal minds. However, it's not possible to do this precisely without some account of the relationship between theory and evidence. Thus, I will briefly introduce an account of theory and evidence drawing on contemporary work in philosophy of science (Section 1.2). We will then proceed in Section 2 to examine research on animal minds in light of this framework.

1.1 Research Aims

One major goal of comparative cognition is to better understand *human* cognition and behavior. For example, biologists and cognitive scientists rely on a wide range of model organisms to understand phenomena such as neurodegenerative disorders in humans. Model organisms are a group of organisms on which a large portion of research is conducted. Examples include the fruit fly (*Drosophila melanogaster*), nematode worm (*C. elegans*), the house mouse (*Mus musculus*), and the brown rat (*Rattus norvegicus*). Consider, for example, the Comparative Cognition Lab led by Jonathon Crystal at Indiana University. Crystal and colleagues examine how rats process and remember events. They've shown that rats appear to use episodic memory to replay a stream of unique events in sequential order, such as a series of odorant experiences (Panoz-Brown et al. 2018). In humans, episodic memory involves remembering events and the context (what, where, when) in which they occur. For example, if I were to ask you to describe what you did this morning, you might "replay" in your imagination the events of the morning in the order in which they occurred (waking up to an alarm, brushing your teeth, etc.). This form of remembering is known as episodic memory or "mental time travel" (Suddendorf & Busby 2003). Episodic memory is impaired in humans with damage to their hippocampus, resulting in amnesia. Individuals suffering from this form of amnesia are described as stuck in time, unable to imagine their personal past, and lacking in "temporal consciousness" (Dalla Barba & La Corte 2013; but see Craver et al. 2014). Crystal and colleagues' research suggests that the hippocampus is crucial for episodic memory in rats as well. When the hippocampal activity in rats is temporarily suppressed, performance on episodic-memory tests is impaired, while other abilities, such as distinguishing between known and unknown odors, is unimpaired. Rats could thus serve as a valuable model of episodic memory, one which might advance our understanding and treatment of human episodic-memory degeneration and impairment, such as that caused by Alzheimer's disease (Crystal 2018, see also Boyle 2020).

In addition to providing insight into human cognition and behavior, comparative cognition informs our understanding of human evolution (MacLean et al. 2012). For example, researchers have examined the communicative abilities of nonhuman primates in an attempt to reconstruct the evolutionary origins of human language. Recent work suggests that great apes, such as chimpanzees and bonobos, use a variety of gestures intentionally and flexibly (Tomasello & Call 2019) and that some of these gestures are novel and acquired over ontogeny (Halina et al. 2013).

Findings such as these have led several research groups to conclude that human language is best understood as evolving from gestural, rather than vocal, communicative practices. For example, Michael Arbib and colleagues argue that pantomime and gestural imitation served as essential scaffolds for the evolution of human language (Arbib et al. 2008). Similarly, based on empirical work on chimpanzees and bonobos, Pollock and de Waal (2007) argue that manual gestures are more promising candidates for the evolution of human language than vocalizations: whereas the vocal signal *scream* is largely invariant in being used in contexts involving threat and attacks, the gesture *gentle touch* is used in a wide range of contexts (travel, mating, grooming) with a range of meanings. As Pika et al. (2007) argue, "since the gestural repertoires of apes are characterized by a high degree of individual variability and flexibility of use as opposed to their vocalizations it seems plausible that gestures were the modality within which symbolic communication first evolved" (p. 41). Despite its ultimate application to humans, research such as this is grounded in an understanding of animal minds. Without a good understanding of gestural communication in chimpanzees, one would lack the grounds necessary to inform theoretical and empirical work on humans.

In addition to studying animal minds for the sake of improving our understanding of humans, however, many comparative cognition researchers are interested in animal minds for their own sake (e.g., see Barron et al. 2023). Researchers working in the domains of *cognitive ecology* and *cognitive ethology* emphasize the role of ecology and evolution in shaping animal minds. Cognitive ecology is a field that aims to integrate knowledge of the natural history of an organism (such as its ecological and evolutionary context) with knowledge of the psychological and neural mechanisms giving rise to that organism's behavior (Healy & Braithwaite 2000). Similarly, the field of cognitive ethology aims to understand how cognitive and behavioral capacities are distributed across the tree of life, as well as their development and adaptiveness (Allen & Bekoff 1997). The focus here is often not on comparing animals with humans, but rather on identifying the diversity of forms cognition takes in organisms exposed to different evolutionary, ecological, and social pressures (Healy & Hurly 2003). Under this approach, one typically starts by observing an organism's behavior in the wild and then seeks to explain that behavior by drawing on what is known about the species' unique ecological context and evolutionary history (Schnell et al. 2021a).

One classic example of this evolutionary and ecological approach concerns food hoarding and spatial cognition. Animals differ in their food hoarding behavior: larder-hoarders stash excess food in one place, scatter-hoarders hide food in multiple places, and nonhoarders do not hoard food at all (Healy et al. 2009). Scatter-hoarders vary in the number of items they cache (from hundreds to thousands) and the length of time before they recover their caches (from a few hours to several months). Some scatter-hoarders even take into account variables like food perishability (e.g., not recovering perishable food items after long intervals) suggesting they know where and when a particular food item (worm versus peanut) was cached (Clayton & Dickinson 1998). Given these behavioral differences, one might expect the spatial cognition of scatter-hoarders and nonhoarders to differ in predictable ways. Indeed, studies suggest that food-hoarding species have better spatial memory than nonhoarding species (Pravosudov & Roth 2013). Similar predictions can be made for species that are distantly related but face similar evolutionary and ecological pressures. For example, great apes and corvids are vertebrates that diverged approximately 300 million years ago, while the coleoid cephalopods (e.g., octopus and cuttlefish) are invertebrates that diverged from vertebrates over 550 million years ago (Figure 1). Like scatter-hoarding corvids, however, cephalopods face many foraging challenges and appear to have the capacity to encode the "what," "where" and "when" features of an event (Jozet-Alves 2013; Schnell et al. 2021b). Thus, the ecological context of a species may provide insight into that species' behavioral profile and cognitive abilities (Amodio et al. 2019). As Healy and Jones (2002) write, "cognitive ecology provides a rationale for the careful formulation and testing of hypotheses" (p. 324).

Some researchers emphasize the importance of studying animals in their natural environment because "it is in this situation that natural selection acts" (Healy & Hurly 2003, p. 326). If cognitive abilities are shaped by the demands of an organism's natural environment, then we might expect to see those abilities on full display in this environment (Boesch 2007). Others counter that conditions which are "unnatural" might guide development and learning in ways that lead to novel cognitive abilities (Tomasello & Call 2008). Great apes raised by humans, for example, develop tool-use and communicative abilities not found in their wild conspecifics. Investigating animals in unusual environments might be particularly important when comparing animals to humans, as many hold that the physical and social environment scaffolds human cognition (Sterelny 2010). Thus, we might not expect to find human-like capacities in other animals unless they are similarly scaffolded.

1.2 Theory and Evidence

Understanding animal minds often requires evaluating cognitive hypotheses in the face of limited and sometimes conflicting data. It is thus helpful to adopt from the outset an account of evidence that we can apply when evaluating

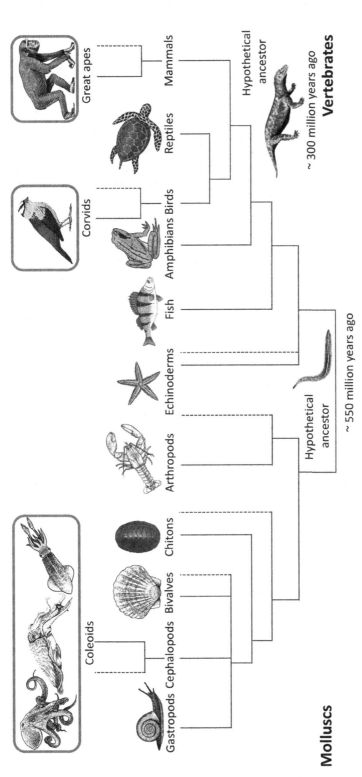

Figure 1 Shared ecological and evolutionary pressures may lead animals to have similar cognitive and behavioral abilities, despite being evolutionarily distantly related. Image from Schnell et al. (2021a).

research in this area. I adopt here the account of evidence advanced by the philosopher of science Julian Reiss (Reiss 2015, 2019). A virtue of Reiss's account is that it emphasizes the importance of local knowledge when evaluating scientific inferences. As we will see, taking a contextual approach toward assessing evidence in comparative cognition will help us make sense of some disagreements in the field and suggest paths toward resolutions.

According to Reiss, a good theory of evidence should distinguish *support* from *warrant*. Providing support for a hypothesis involves collecting facts that are relevant to that hypothesis. Like a detective collecting information pertaining to an investigation, scientists collect data pertaining to a hypothesis. However, such collections are not the same as inferring whether to accept a hypothesis. One can gather information without "making up one's mind" in this way (Reiss 2015, p. 353). A hypothesis is warranted, on the other hand, when a decision has been made about whether to accept or infer it. According to Reiss, a theory of evidence should account for both parts of this process. With respect to warrant, it should tell us: Out of the relevant facts we've collected, which ones and how many are needed to warrant the hypothesis under investigation? Let us briefly unpack the concepts of support and warrant before examining how they work in practice in comparative cognition. We will appeal to both concepts throughout this Element.

Reiss distinguishes between two kinds of support: direct and indirect. Evidence e_d provides *direct support* for some target hypothesis h "if and only if e_d is a pattern in the data we are entitled to expect to obtain under the supposition that h is true" (Reiss 2015, p. 347). Evidence e_i provides *indirect support* for h "if and only if e_i is a pattern in the data that is incompatible with what we are entitled to expect to obtain under the supposition of the truth of one of h's alternative hypotheses h', h'', h''', and so on" (Reiss 2015, p. 347). Alternative hypotheses are those that differ from the target hypothesis but can also explain the empirical data. Such alternatives need to be empirically plausible, given our background knowledge, in order to be relevant. As Reiss writes, "In the context of scientific inquiry it would be inappropriate to advance a general skeptical alternative, such as an evil-demon hypothesis" (2015, p. 351). One eliminates an alternative hypothesis by citing data that is incompatible with what we would expect under the supposition that this alternative hypothesis is true, thus providing indirect support for the target hypothesis. Crucially, one cannot eliminate an alternative hypothesis with "objective certainty." Instead, one must make a judgment in light of one's background knowledge and values: "If little hinges on the decision, we may keep entertaining an alternative even in light of dramatic indirect support" (Reiss 2015, p. 353).

The above definitions of support provide an answer to the question, "what information is relevant for evaluating a hypothesis?" It provides a guide regarding what information we should seek to collect. However, it is important to note that what we are "entitled to expect" depends on contextual factors such as the background knowledge of a community (Reiss 2015, 2019). It is here where local knowledge becomes critical for evaluating hypotheses. Consider, for example, the causal hypothesis, "x causes y." What one is entitled to expect under the assumption that this hypothesis is true will depend on one's background knowledge about how causes work. For example, although probabilistic causality is widely accepted today, a century ago views of causality were deterministic (Reiss 2015, p. 350). Thus, although today we may be entitled to expect a pattern in the data in which x leads to y probabilistically, given the hypothesis "x causes y," this may not have been the case a century ago, and thus would not qualify as support for the hypothesis.[2]

As noted, a hypothesis is warranted when it has met our criteria regarding the level of direct and indirect support needed to infer it. According to Reiss, warrant comes in degrees, and the degree to which a hypothesis is warranted depends on the level of direct and indirect support available. First, to have any warrant at all, a hypothesis must have some direct support (this is a necessary condition). The degree of warrant then depends on the indirect support available for the hypothesis. A hypothesis has empirical or inductive "proof" when *all* alternative accounts have been eliminated. Note this is not a case of deductive proof: it depends on the available evidence and alternative hypotheses under consideration. As our theories, evidence, background knowledge, etc. change, so might our view that a hypothesis is warranted in this way. A hypothesis has "strong warrant" when all salient alternatives have been eliminated, as well as some alternatives that are nonsalient. A salient alternative is one that itself has direct support. Finally, a hypothesis has "moderate warrant" when most alternatives have been eliminated (including some salient alternatives) and "weak warrant" when only some alternatives have been eliminated (Table 1).

Reiss's general account of evidence fits comparative cognition well. Comparative cognition researchers regularly engage in formulating and eliminating alternative hypotheses and take this to be a central step in providing warrant for a cognitive hypothesis (where a cognitive hypothesis is a claim about the psychological or neural mechanisms responsible for a suite of behaviors). For example, Schnell et al. (2021a) identify three key steps to warranting cognitive hypotheses in comparative cognition: First, identify the relevant

---

[2] See de Regt (2017) for additional historical examples of how changing background knowledge affects what researchers take to count as good scientific explanations.

Table 1 To have any warrant at all, a hypothesis must have direct support. The degree of warrant is then determined by the level of indirect support. Table from Reiss (2015, p. 358).

Different Grades of Warrant

Grade	Name	Direct Support Plus Indirect Support That ...
1	Proof	Eliminates all (relevant) alternative accounts
2	Strong warrant	Eliminates all salient alternative accounts and some that are nonsalient
3	Moderate warrant	Eliminates most alternatives, including some that are salient
4	Weak warrant	Eliminates some alternative accounts

behavior to be cognitively explained (e.g., food caching). Second, formulate behavioral criteria for the hypothesized cognitive ability (such as episodic memory). Third, rule out any alternative hypotheses that can explain the observed behavior. The second and third steps correspond to gathering direct and indirect evidence. Similarly, Cecilia Heyes describes the "method of testing alternative hypotheses" as key to the study of animal minds (Heyes 2008). This strategy involves using experiments to evaluate two or more explanations for a given behavior in order to choose between them. According to Heyes, this method of testing alternative hypotheses is required for making well-evidenced claims about the cognitive capacities of animals.

With this theory of evidence in hand, let us now examine how comparative cognition researchers investigate whether animals reason about unobservable variables. How this claim is evaluated depends in part on the particular unobservable variable being considered. In what follows, I will focus on two examples commonly discussed in the literature: causal reasoning and mindreading. As we will see, many researchers characterize causal reasoning as reasoning about unobservable physical variables (such as weight and force) and mindreading as reasoning about unobservable mental states (such as desire and belief).

2 Animal Minds: Empirical Investigations

2.1 Causal Reasoning

A major research program in comparative cognition is dedicated to determining whether nonhuman animals engage in causal reasoning. Studies in this research paradigm often start by observing that humans reason about unobservable causes. For example, Civelek et al. (2020) write, "Human adults can infer unseen causes because they represent the events around them in terms of their underlying causal mechanisms" (p. 1). Blaisdell et al. (2006) also note, "The ability to acquire and reason with causal knowledge is among our most central human cognitive competences" (p. 1020). The question then is whether other animals reason about unobservable causes as well, and if so, how. The world contains a variety of causes and causal regularities: heavy things fall to the ground, water is displaced by sinking (rather than floating) objects, some objects can be used to displace or dislodge others, etc. An agent capable of causal reasoning should recognize some of the causal factors underlying these situations and use them to solve problems. Such an agent would also be able to transfer knowledge acquired in one situation to another causally equivalent situation, even if the two situations differ in their noncausal properties (e.g., a heavy object will succeed in displacing water, regardless of whether the object is made of stone or metal) (Seed et al. 2011).

How do researchers provide *direct support* for causal reasoning in nonhuman animals? Broadly, they give animals a causal or physical problem-solving task. Often the problem involves obtaining desirable food, thus participants are motivated to solve it. For example, a common paradigm used to test for causal reasoning is the trap-tube task. In this task, participants are presented with a transparent tube that contains a reward. To extract the reward, participants must use a tool (e.g., a stick) or a body part (such as a finger) to push or pull the reward out of the tube. However, the tube also contains one or more "traps." The traps are designed such that if the food item were to fall into a trap during the process of extraction, it would be irretrievable. Figure 2 shows a standard trap-tube task.

The idea behind the trap-tube task is that agents with the capacity for causal reasoning will avoid the functional traps thereby succeeding in extracting the food reward. In other words, if the hypothesis that chimpanzees have causal reasoning is true, then a chimpanzee facing this task should avoid pushing or pulling the food toward the opening of a trap because she will know that 1) objects left unsupported from below fall, 2) once fallen, objects do not defy gravity and emerge from containers on their own, 3) objects do not penetrate solid surfaces, so the food will not fall through the bottom of the trap, etc. In this way, the trap-tube task probes participants' understanding of solidity, surfaces, and gravity. Other causal-reasoning tasks are designed to probe these, as well as other, aspects of causal reasoning. For example, "string-pulling" tasks examine participants' understandings of contact and connection (Jacobs & Osvath 2015); "Aesop's Fable" tasks (noted in the Introduction) examine conceptions of weight, solidity, and displacement (Jelbert et al. 2015); platform-pushing tasks examine conceptions of contact and force (von Bayern et al. 2009); etc.

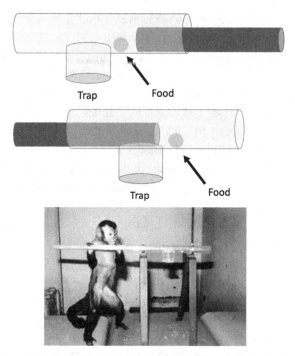

Figure 2 A standard trap-tube task consisting of a transparent plastic tube, food, and a trap positioned at the bottom of the tube (see Visalberghi & Limongelli 1994). Top: A potential failed attempt. If the stick is pushed, the food will fall into the trap. Middle: A potential successful attempt. If the stick is pushed, the food will fall out of the tube and will be retrievable by the participant. Bottom: A capuchin monkey engaging in a trap-tube task (from Visalberghi & Tomasello 1998).

Success on tasks such as these is what researchers expect of an individual animal on the assumption that this individual is capable of causal reasoning. This is only a small step toward gathering support for a given causal-reasoning hypothesis, however. Comparative cognition researchers spend a majority of their time ensuring that they have gathered sufficient *indirect support* for the target hypothesis. The reason for this is that there are numerous alternative hypotheses that can explain successful performance on a problem-solving task. In experimental work, these alternative hypotheses take the form of "extraneous" variables. Extraneous variables are those variables (other than the independent variable) that could affect the dependent variable. The independent variable is what researchers manipulate in an experiment in order to determine its effects, while the dependent variable is what researchers measure. The aim of an experiment is to test whether and how the independent variable affects the dependent variable. To do this, one must control for the "noise" created by extraneous variables because the effects of the independent variable can be lost or washed out in this noise. Researchers control for extraneous variables through experimental design and inferential statistics (Bausman & Halina 2018; Dacey 2023). For example, in the case of the trap-tube task, the independent variable is a participant's capacity for causal reasoning and the dependent variable is whether that participant successfully retrieves the reward by avoiding the traps. There are, however, extraneous variables that can lead to successful performance on a trap-tube task independently of causal reasoning: for example, participants might avoid a trap because they have formed a negative association with its shape or color, rather than because they understand its causal properties as a trap. These extraneous variables constitute "alternative accounts" as discussed in Section 1. Eliminating them as plausible accounts for successful performance on trap-tube tasks is required to obtain moderate or strong warrant for the hypothesis that an animal's success on such tasks depends on causal reasoning.

Comparative cognition researchers work hard to control for extraneous variables through good experimental design and statistical analysis. However, in doing so, they face an additional unique challenge: the participants in their studies are what I will call "clever black boxes." Animals are *clever* in the sense that they often have extraordinary sensory capacities (hearing, sight, smell, etc.), exceptional learning capacities (such as the ability to quickly associate cues with rewards), and many other internal capacities that support problem solving (such as species-specific predispositions to direct attention in ways that facilitate learning). Animals are *black boxes* in the sense that we often lack an understanding of the capacities that give rise to their behavior. These capacities are something that researchers can infer over time based on theoretical and empirical considerations. However, they are grounded in the complex internal workings of an animal's body and nervous system, and thus are initially hidden from us, like the interior of an opaque box. Given the clever black box nature of animals, it is difficult and sometimes impossible to control for all extraneous variables. The less we know about an animal's internal capacities, the more likely it is that they have solved a task in a way unanticipated by researchers. The classic case of Clever Hans illustrates this challenge well. Many take the case of Clever Hans as illustrating the negative epistemic effects of poorly controlled research. However, few highlight that Hans gave rise to unanticipated extraneous variables in virtue of his clever black box nature. It is worth briefly considering this historical case before examining more closely the indirect support available for causal reasoning in animals.

Clever Hans was a horse living in Berlin at the turn of the twentieth century who became famous for his ability to answer questions on a wide range of topics – from mathematics to music theory to reading German.[3] Hans responded to questions by tapping his hoof, nodding and shaking his head, or pointing to objects with his nose to indicate answers to questions. Moreover, Hans' answers were often correct. Eventually, the biologist and psychologist Oskar Pfungst discovered that Hans was answering questions correctly not because he understood them and knew the answers, but rather because he was picking up on social cues from the questioner or human observers. The lesson drawn from this historical episode is often that comparative cognition researchers must be careful not to interpret animal behavior anthropomorphically (i.e., as we would interpret human behavior) and must instead be extremely careful to control for extraneous variables (in this case, social cues). This lesson, however, suggests that prior to the work of Pfungst, those engaging Hans were being scientifically sloppy or naïve, eager to attribute human-like cognitive abilities to Hans, when the implementation of a few experimental controls would have made it clear that this was a poor inference. In fact, at the time, many researchers tried to show that Hans' abilities must be the result of some "trick" but failed to do so. It was only after extensive testing that researchers like the naturalist C. G. Schillings and psychologist Carl Stumpf (founder of the Berlin School of Experimental Psychology and a former student of Franz Brentano) began to accept that Hans' responses might be genuine. Pfungst also had great difficulty determining the source of Hans' answers. Working with Hans, Pfungst learned to his surprise that he could cause Hans to choose the wrong answer by "focussing consciousness, with a great degree of intensity, upon the answer desired," but he didn't know how Hans was detecting this state of consciousness (Pfungst 1911/2010, p. 90). Ultimately, Pfungst found that Hans had learned (without explicit training) to track bodily states of tension in people. As Trestman (2015) writes, "it was primarily through careful introspective analysis of the feelings of tension (i.e., that they manifested in part as feelings of tension in the head and neck), that Pfungst was finally able to isolate the postural cues that Hans was using" (p. 90). Moreover, Hans could rely on postural cues from audience members when the questioner was not visible, and could rely on such cues even when performing in a variety of different noisy and crowded settings. Finally, if these cues were unavailable (e.g., if he could not see around his blinders), Hans would shake his head until he could see or refuse to participate in the question-and-answer session (Trestman 2015, p. 89).

---

[3] For the following account of Clever Hans, I draw on Trestman (2015).

As noted, the case of Clever Hans is often used to show how epistemic principles can help researchers avoid mistakes. Currie (2021), for example, writes, "Horses being sensitive to human body language is less surprising than horses being able to count and do sums" (p. 34); given this, we should prefer the former explanation over the latter. This, however, doesn't capture the case of Clever Hans in its historical nuance.[4] Despite their knowledge of horse behavior, skilled biologists and psychologists of the time did not anticipate that Hans would be able to rely on the cluster of abilities described above (sensitivity to extremely subtle and involuntary cues from different people in noisy settings, etc.). This was an "unconceived alternative" (Stanford 2006) and it took some time for Pfungst to piece together a viable alternative explanation for Hans' behavior. The lesson to draw from this episode instead is that some alternative explanations remain unconceived at the time of research. In the case of comparative cognition, this is particularly the case when we lack sufficient background knowledge of the animal under study. In other words, insofar as researchers lack knowledge of an animal's cognitive capacities, there are likely unconceived alternatives that could explain that animal's behavior on a given task. Researchers wanting to know more about animal minds thus face a Catch-22: having warrant for a hypothesis requires eliminating alternative hypotheses, but it is difficult to conceive of all plausible alternatives without knowing more about the cognitive abilities of the animal (e.g., their sensory, memory, learning, and other abilities). With hindsight, we might find it plausible that horses can engage in subtle posture reading, etc., but without this knowledge, researchers are likely to fail to control for this alternative. The fact that animals are clever black boxes means we sometimes cannot anticipate and control for the many means by which they might succeed at a given task. The more knowledge we have of a given animal's abilities, the better we can anticipate and control for plausible alternatives.

Returning to causal reasoning in animals, what alternative accounts do researchers typically aim to eliminate? They typically aim to eliminate the alternative hypothesis that participants are solving a task through some form of associative learning. Broadly, associative learning is the ability to learn associations between stimuli like a bell and food (classical conditioning) or between actions and outcomes like receiving food upon pressing a lever (operant conditioning). One justification for treating associative learning as a salient alternative hypothesis is that it is phylogenetically widespread. If associative learning is phylogenetically widespread, it's reasonable to assume that the

---

[4] In fairness to Currie, he presents this not as a historical example, but rather anachronistically to illustrate the epistemic principle of parsimony in action.

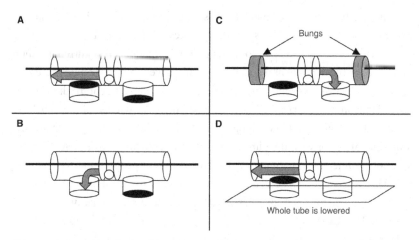

Figure 3 A series of transfer tasks conducted by Seed et al. (2006) on rooks (*Corvus frugilegus*). These tasks are designed to eliminate the possibility that rooks are solving causal problems through the learned association of cues, rather than causal reasoning.

organism being tested has this capacity and will use it when possible to solve the problem at hand (Sober 2012; but see Meketa 2014). To eliminate this alternative explanation, researchers typically implement various "transfer tasks" designed to distinguish the bona fide casual reasoner from the associative learner. Broadly, a transfer task is a task used to determine whether and how an animal's capacities or skills vary across contexts.

For example, Figure 3 illustrates a series of transfer tasks given to rooks to eliminate several associative-learning alternatives for successful performance on these tasks. In this study, participants could move the reward (depicted as a circle in the middle of the tube in Figure 3) left or right by pulling on a stick (the bold black line). The stick is connected to two clear plastic discs enclosing the reward; thus, pulling on the stick rakes the food out of the tube or into a trap, depending on whether one has chosen to pull left or right. In the figure, the arrow depicts the solution and all tubes and traps are open unless they end in bungs, a black disc, or the ground (in the case of Tube D). Note that a participant might solve Tube A in Figure 3 by learning the cue-based rule "pass the reward over the black surface." However, this rule cannot be used to successfully solve Tube B. Thus, a participant who performs well on both Tubes A and B is likely not relying on this cue-based rule. However, such a participant might be relying on the associatively learned rule "avoid the hole with the black disc at the bottom" (Seed et al. 2006, p. 698). Following this rule would allow one to avoid the trap in both Tubes A and B. Tubes C and D are thus introduced to test this alternative account. In these two cases, there are no holes with black discs at the bottom to avoid. Instead, in Tube C, bungs are introduced: moving the food left is now ineffective due to the lack of an opening. And in Tube D, the whole apparatus is lowered to the ground: moving the food right in this case results in the food being trapped because it can no longer be retrieved from below. Passing transfer tasks like these is taken as indirect support for the hypothesis that an agent is relying on causal reasoning: it indicates that the successful agent is not relying on an ability to associate cues to solve the tasks. In this way, researchers eliminate what they take to be a salient alternative hypothesis to the claim that animals reason about unobservable causes, such as gravity.

Despite implementing experimental controls like these in trap-tube and other causal reasoning tasks, there is currently no consensus regarding the level of warrant for the hypothesis that nonhuman animals engage in causal reasoning. In the case of great apes such as chimpanzees, some researchers hold that there is warrant for this hypothesis (Völter et al. 2016; Claudio et al. 2019), while others disagree (see Hanus 2016 for discussion). In the case of corvids, like New Caledonian Crows, some researchers again think there is warrant for causal reasoning (Jelbert et al. 2019), while others disagree (see Taylor 2020; Vonk 2020). Typically, when researchers disagree that there is strong or moderate warrant for a causal-reasoning hypothesis, it is because they think existing studies have failed to eliminate some alternative associative-learning hypothesis (although see Section 2.3).

A similar dynamic is found in other research areas dedicated to testing animals' abilities to reason about unobservable variables. As Starzak and Gray (2021) note, "Over and over again the familiar refrain is, 'do animals have complex human-like cognitive abilities or can their behavior be explained in terms of simpler processes such as associative learning?'" (p. 2). We will briefly examine one more example of this dialectic in the next section before turning in Section 2.3 to a general criticism advanced against mainstream experimental approaches in comparative cognition.

2.2 Mindreading

Mindreading (also referred to as "theory of mind") is broadly the ability to attribute mental states to other agents, such as intentions, perceptions, and desires. Like causal reasoning studies, research on mindreading in animals often begins with the observation that humans predict and explain behavior based on the attribution of unobservable mental states. For example, Kaminski (2015) writes: "Human social cognition is unique because humans can, in some situations, make predictions about others' mental states … Whether other primates also have the ability to attribute mental states to others is a highly debated question" (p. 1741). Similarly, Krupenye (2016) write: "Central to everything that makes us human – including our distinctive modes of communication, cooperation, and culture – is our theory of mind" (p. 110). There is no consensus regarding how exactly humans generate mental-state attributions, but there is a consensus that we often predict and explain behavior by attributing unobservable mental states to other agents, and that these predictions and explanations are regularly successful (but see Andrews 2012).

Comparative cognition researchers have dedicated a major strand of research to determining whether other animals engage in human-like mind-reading. These studies often follow a similar structure to those used for identifying mindreading in humans through nonverbal means. For example, Krupenye et al. (2016) tested whether nonhuman great apes pass implicit false belief tasks. Broadly, a false belief task tests for mindreading abilities by determining whether one attributes false beliefs (or beliefs that are incongruent with reality) to other agents. Often false belief tasks rely on explicit judgments. For example, a researcher might ask a participant, "where will Sally look for her marble?" and "where is the marble really?" in a case where Sally has a false belief about the marble's location (see Baron-Cohen et al. 1985). Participants must correctly answer these questions through pointing or verbal report to pass this task. However, explicit false belief tasks are thought to be cognitively demanding, potentially requiring advanced language and executive functions (Devine & Hughes 2014). In contrast, implicit false belief tasks measure whether participants show implicit signs of tracking false beliefs, rather than explicit judgments like verbal reports. One often-used implicit measure for testing false-belief understanding in human infants and young children is anticipatory looking. In the Sally case, rather than asking participants "where will Sally look for her marble?" researchers measure where participants will look in anticipation of Sally searching for her marble. The idea is that if participants have implicit mindreading abilities, they will look at the location where Sally falsely believes the object is located (rather than where the object is actually located).

Following the above anticipatory-looking paradigm, Krupenye and colleagues tracked the gaze of chimpanzees, bonobos, and orangutans as they watched videos of competitive encounters between a human and an apelike character ("King Kong"). In one experiment (Figure 4), King Kong steals a stone from a human and hides it in one of two boxes (say, Box 1). King Kong then threatens the human upon which the human leaves the room. While the human is gone, King Kong moves the stone from Box 1 to Box 2; he then

Figure 4 A false-belief task designed for testing mindreading (specifically, the ability to attribute false beliefs) in great apes. Participants watch videos depicting competitive social interactions such as the one shown here. Following studies on humans, researchers use anticipatory looking to determine where participants expect another agent believes an object is located. Image from Krupenye et al. (2016).

removes the stone from Box 2 and leaves the scene entirely with the stone. Finally, the human returns to the room and approaches the boxes. The question is where will participants anticipate the human will look for the stolen stone? If participants attribute a false belief to the human, they should expect them to reach for Box 1 where they last saw King Kong place the object (despite the fact that the object is no longer there). If participants instead attribute to the human the belief that the stone is gone (as it in fact is), then they should not anticipate that the human will reach for Box 1.

As in causal reasoning research, in mindreading studies, researchers state in advance how they expect subjects will behave on the assumption that the mindreading hypothesis is true. For example, the experiment by Krupenye and colleagues is designed to probe whether participants will behave as if they are attributing false beliefs. Following studies on humans, researchers reason that, in this situation, attributions of false belief will result in a specific outcome regarding looking behavior: namely, looking at the location where the agent with the false belief wrongly expects the object to be (Box 1 in the above example). If this outcome is observed, then this constitutes direct evidence for the mindreading hypothesis under investigation. If subjects fail to exhibit the predicted behavioral pattern, then the experiment fails to support the mindreading hypothesis (but see Section 3). In the study by Krupenye and colleagues, great apes behaved as predicted by the mindreading hypothesis.

In the case of mindreading research, the analysis of indirect support also resembles studies on causal reasoning. Researchers are careful to control for alternative associative learning hypotheses. The exact form that a plausible alternative hypothesis takes depends on the structure and features of the experiment. For example, in the above implicit false belief task, Krupenye et al. (2016) write, "Apes were never shown the actor's search behavior when he held a false belief, precluding reliance on external behavioral cues learned during the task" (p. 113). They also note that the scenarios were designed to be novel to participants, thus making it unlikely that the behavior of subjects was a product of behavioral rules learned from previous experience. After eliminating plausible alternative explanations, the authors conclude that nonhuman great apes have an implicit understanding of false beliefs and thus that this cognitive ability is "likely at least as old as humans' last common ancestor with the other apes" (Krupenye et al. 2016, p. 113).

Consistent with Reiss's account of evidence outlined above, background knowledge plays a crucial role in establishing warrant for a hypothesis in comparative cognition. First, researchers must determine what they are entitled to expect on the assumption that their target hypothesis is true. In the case of causal reasoning and mindreading, these expectations are formed in large part based on prior research on humans. For example, Krupenye and colleagues write that their "design, controls, and general procedure" was based on a seminal implicit false belief task designed for human infants (2016, p. 111). The seminal study was one conducted by Victoria Southgate and colleagues on human 2-year-olds. Based on looking times, Southgate and colleagues found that children anticipate another person's behavior in accordance with that person's false belief (Southgate et al. 2007). Southgate's study in turn was based on other studies using a similar paradigm to study mindreading in infants (e.g., Onishi & Baillargeon 2005; Surian et al. 2007). Southgate and colleagues take their own positive results as corroborating these previous studies. Thus, the predictions that Krupenye and colleagues make regarding how great apes will behave on the assumption that they attribute false beliefs draws on an emerging consensus (in this case, in developmental psychology) regarding how mind-reading should affect looking time in particular contexts (but see Kampis et al. 2021).

The second way background knowledge features in establishing warrant concerns identifying alternative hypotheses and determining their level of salience. As we have seen, comparative cognition researchers control for numerous alternative hypotheses when conducting their studies. Some of these controls are standard across the experimental sciences: for example, randomizing subjects to control for extraneous variables like age, sex, and rearing history. Others are specific to the phenomenon under investigation. Associative learning is considered a salient alternative hypothesis in causal reasoning and mindreading research, but this hypothesis takes many forms, as animals can learn to associate many different cues in many different ways (which cues they associate further depends on their learning history and factors like innate predispositions (Versace et al. 2018)). One must draw on this background knowledge to determine which alternative hypotheses need eliminating, given the experimental setup. Moreover, different researchers bring different background knowledge to bear on this problem. Often it is not until a study is published that additional alternative explanations emerge (particularly from those who are specialists in associative learning). For example, in response to Krupenye and colleagues' study above, the experimental psychologist Cecilia Heyes published a response proposing the alternative hypothesis that when the human returns to look for the brick, the green color of their shirt might have activated a memory (in the participant) of where the brick was when the green shirt was last seen (Heyes 2017; see also Heyes 2014a, 2014b). Under this interpretation, great apes in this study do not behave as they do because of mindreading, but rather due to learned associations between the spatial config-uration of objects (green shirt, boxes, brick) and target locations (where the brick was when the green shirt was present). This proposed alternative (con-ceived by Heyes due to her expertise on associative learning) then led Krupenye and colleagues to conduct further tests to attempt to eliminate this alternative (see Krupenye et al. 2017; Kano et al. 2017).

The above dynamic can be a fruitful one. As we saw in the case of Clever Hans, it is challenging to conceive of plausible alternatives, particularly when one's knowledge of the cognitive capacities of an animal is limited. One research team is unlikely to have the background knowledge necessary to conceive of all plausible alternative hypotheses. By drawing on the knowledge of the broader community, one has greater assurance that relevant alternative hypotheses have been formulated and eliminated, thereby increasing the strength of the warrant for the target hypothesis. That said, as we will see in Section 3, debates in comparative cognition reveal that there is a tradeoff between the number of alternative hypotheses available (and the ease by which researchers are able to generate these alternatives) and the strength of warrant one is likely to obtain for a target hypothesis. In research on causal reasoning and mindreading, there is a profusion of alternative hypotheses, making it unlikely that researchers will obtain strong warrant for these target hypotheses. Before turning to this tradeoff, however, let's consider a critique of comparative cognition that has featured prominently in the literature. Engaging this critique provides additional insight into the challenges involved in investigating animal minds and potential directions forward.

2.3 The Relational Reinterpretation (RR) Hypothesis

Over the last twenty years, the psychologist Daniel Povinelli and colleagues have advanced what they view as a devastating criticism of research on animal minds (for a description, see Povinelli 2020). They call their view the "relational reinterpretation (RR) hypothesis" because it posits that only humans reinterpret the world in terms of higher-order relations (more on this below). Framed in terms of Reiss's theory of evidence, we can articulate their view as follows: 1) the majority of researchers are consistently mistaken about the pattern of data one is entitled to expect under the assumption that the hypothesis h (e.g., that animals reason about unobservable variables) is true and 2) the majority of researchers are consistently mistaken about the salient alternative accounts that need to be eliminated in order to infer h. Note that if Povinelli and colleagues are correct, this is indeed a major problem for a vast amount of work in comparative cognition. It would mean researchers are mistaken about what counts as direct and indirect support for h. In this case, the resources that have gone into gathering support for h thus far (numerous studies on causal reasoning and mindreading, for instance) are in fact incapable of providing warrant for h. Thus, there is not only "no evidence" for the claim that animals like chimpanzees engage in causal reasoning or mindreading, but the current experimental approach (illustrated above) is unable to produce such evidence even in principle (Penn & Povinelli 2007; Povinelli & Penn 2011). In this section, I briefly reconstruct the position of Povinelli and colleagues. Then, in the following section, I evaluate their claims, arguing that although the RR hypothesis may be worth pursuing, this does not entail that mainstream research approaches are mistaken. Indeed, a virtue of mainstream approaches is their flexibility regarding what counts as the phenomenon of interest (something the approach advocated by Povinelli and colleagues lacks).

Povinelli and colleagues build their case by first noting that both human and nonhuman animals can form many abstract representations about observable features, objects, and relations in the world. Humans regularly form abstract concepts like *apple, cup,* and *animal.* Similarly, chimpanzees readily identify other chimpanzees as chimpanzees or conspecifics, despite individual chimpanzees differing widely in physical appearance and behavior (from young infants to adults, for example).[5] How do human and nonhuman animals form such categories or concepts? According to Povinelli and colleagues, they do so by drawing on the observable features that members of each category have in common. These shared features need not be simple or obvious; individuals in a category may have few observable features in common. But the idea is that one can depend on such shared observable features to form abstract categories because the members of the class are observable. Povinelli and colleagues refer to such categories as "first-order representations," "first-order perceptual relations," "perceptual relations," "perceptual abstractions," or "perceptual symbols" (Penn et al. 2008; Povinelli & Penn 2011; Povinelli 2020). In Povinelli's (2020) words, these can be understood as a "*many-to-one* mapping of sensory inputs onto mental representations that can cope with the superficial differences of particular situations" (p. 591, emphasis original). According to Povinelli, humans and other animals both readily form such perceptual abstractions.

Although nonhuman animals share with humans the ability to form perceptual abstractions, only humans have the additional ability to form abstract representations of *unobservable* features, objects, and relations, according to Povinelli and colleagues. Humans can form abstract concepts such as *ghost* or *god* despite never having observed a ghost or a god. According to the RR hypothesis, the ability to engage in causal reasoning and mindreading requires reasoning about unobservable variables such as these. Causal reasoning requires thinking about abstract concepts such as *force, weight,* and *gravity;* mindreading requires thinking about abstract concepts such as *goals, beliefs,* and *knowledge.* These are abstract representations of unobservable features, objects, and relations and thus require "higher-order" rather than "first-order" representations (Penn et al. 2008; Povinelli 2020). These representations are

---

[5] There is of course an important question regarding *how* chimpanzees conceptualize other chimpanzees (see Allen 1992 for discussion). When researchers say that a chimpanzee identifies another agent as a "chimpanzee," they do not mean that they have a human-like concept of "chimpanzee" (conceptualizing them as members of the species *Pan troglodytes,* for instance), but rather, as potential mates, adversaries, grooming partners, etc.

higher order because they represent relations among relations. For example, one might categorize objects on the basis of their observable properties, such as color, size, texture, or smell. A higher-order representation would further pick out the relations among these relations: one would be able to identify "sameness" in one category of things (say colors) as like "sameness" in another category of things (say size). According to the RR hypothesis, the latter is required for reasoning about unobservable variables like causes and mental states, and only humans have this ability. As Vonk and Povinelli (2012) write, "whereas many species form concepts about observable things and use those concepts in flexible and productive ways, humans alone think about such things as God, ghosts, gravity, and other minds" (p. 555). The idea is that the members of such categories are perceptually disparate, sharing only higher-order properties, such as invisibility. Invisibility is not one observable property that ghosts have in common, but an abstract functional regularity – a suite of behaviors about how ghost people or ghost cats will behave and lead others to behave, given their invisibility. To think about "God, ghosts, gravity, and other minds" thus requires representing relations among relations, according to this view.

It is the combination of these two claims (that nonhuman animals readily form perceptual abstractions and humans additionally reason about unobservables) that leads to Povinelli and colleagues' criticism of research on animal minds. They argue that the existing results on causal reasoning and mindreading tasks can be explained by appealing to the ability to form perceptual abstractions. Indeed, perceptual abstractions are *necessary and sufficient* for the observed behavior of animals on these tasks. They are necessary because animals without first-order representations wouldn't be able to engage (much less succeed) in many of these tasks. For example, one must be able to group together events such as "eyes visible" and "eyes not visible" to succeed in many tasks aimed at testing the attribution of perceptual states (such as "seeing" and "not seeing"). Regardless of whether one is capable of mindreading, the capacity to engage in these kinds of perceptual abstractions is required to participate in a mindreading task: "There is no way to control away the very perceptual stimuli that are purported to connect the animal to the task" (Povinelli 2020, p. 608; see also Povinelli & Vonk 2004; Vonk & Povinelli 2012). Povinelli and colleagues go on to argue that all successful performance on causal reasoning and mindreading tasks can be explained by appealing to such first-order abstract representations. For example, successful performance in the Krupenye et al. false belief task discussed above (see Figure 4) can be explained as follows: participants will expect another agent to look for objects in the location where they were when the agent was last present. This requires categorizing together situations like "object location when agent present" versus "object location when agent not present," but these categories are based on observable properties and thus count as perceptual abstractions according to the RR hypothesis. Povinelli et al. further hold that all studies aimed to test an animal's ability to reason about unobservable variables can be explained by appealing to perceptual abstractions in this way. Thus, there is no reason to posit the additional ability of reasoning about higher-order representations. Such higher-order states, *"do no causal work above and beyond that already specified by first-order states"* (Povinelli 2020, p. 593, emphasis original).

Although mainstream researchers believe they're providing evidence for *h* when eliminating associative learning alternatives, it is not these alternative hypotheses that matter, according to Povinelli and colleagues. One must instead eliminate the alternative that animals solve tasks using perceptual abstractions. However, researchers cannot do this because their experiments depend on animals using such perceptual abstractions. Eliminating this salient alternative requires a different experimental paradigm entirely.

To summarize, according to Povinelli and colleagues, most comparative cognition researchers fail to fully appreciate that causal reasoning and mindreading require higher-order reasoning or the ability to categorize entities, features, and relations according to, for example, their functional roles despite having no perceptual features in common. Were researchers to recognize this crucial point, they would also recognize that the studies conducted thus far fail to provide evidence for reasoning about unobservable variables, because these studies have consistently failed to eliminate the alternative hypothesis that participants rely on perceptual abstractions alone. Indeed, perceptual abstraction is not a hypothesis that researchers currently recognize as a salient alternative at all; thus, they are "doomed to failure" in their attempt to empirically investigate causal reasoning and mindreading in nonhuman animals (Povinelli 2020, p. 589). This argument can be summarized as follows:

Premise 1	Reasoning about causes and mental states is a form of reasoning about unobservable variables
Premise 2	Reasoning about unobservable variables requires higher-order reasoning
Premise 3	In order to provide evidence for higher-order reasoning, one must eliminate the salient alternative hypothesis that an agent is engaging in perceptual abstraction
Premise 4	Current experiments fail to eliminate perceptual abstraction as a salient alternative
Conclusion	Current experiments do not provide evidence for reasoning about unobservable variables such as causes and mental states

In the next section (Section 3.1), I argue against premise 2. Rejecting this premise means that one need not eliminate perceptual abstraction as an alternative hypothesis to provide evidence for the hypothesis that animals reason about causes and mental states. The general upshot is that there is room for disagreement regarding the nature of phenomena like mindreading and causal reasoning, and any such disagreement affects what we take as evidence for these phenomena. Having rejected Povinelli and colleagues' critique of mainstream approaches in comparative cognition, I then return in Section 3.2 to these approaches, highlighting what I take to be their major strengths and weaknesses.

3 Problems with Existing Approaches

Focusing on just the human case, should we understand capacities such as causal reasoning and mindreading in the way that Povinelli and colleagues do? Crucially, Povinelli's account is only one out of many available accounts and it is not clearly the most theoretically or empirically plausible account advanced in the literature, or so I shall argue. This does not mean we should reject the RR hypothesis entirely, but it does mean that Povinelli and colleagues are mistaken in claiming that we should reject *all other accounts* in favor of their approach or that "the approaches deployed by comparative psychologists are doomed to failure" (Povinelli 2020, p. 589). A fruitful research program should entertain multiple hypotheses, particularly when in the early stages of research. Such an approach is consistent with other successful research program in biology and the cognitive sciences. Thus, Povinelli and colleagues should advance their hypothesis as one among many, but using the RR hypothesis to undermine alternative research strategies is unjustified and detrimental to empirical work.

3.1 Problems with the RR Hypothesis

As we saw in Section 1, comparative cognition researchers regularly describe mindreading and causal reasoning as capacities that involve attributing "unobservable" states to others. Thus, we can grant that describing a mental state or causal mechanism as "unobservable" is something that researchers widely accept. The RR hypothesis additionally holds that reasoning about unobservables *requires* higher-order reasoning (premise 2 above). We saw in the previous section that higher-order reasoning is the alleged ability to categorize entities based on their higher-order relations or relations among relations (e.g., identifying similar colors and similar shapes as belonging to the same category because they share the relational property of similarity, rather than properties like being blue or square). But why do Povinelli and colleagues hold that reasoning about unobservables requires such higher-order reasoning? They give both an empirical reason and an analytic reason for doing so. In this section, I briefly evaluate these two reasons, finding neither ultimately convincing. The upshot is that the RR hypothesis is not as compelling as its advocates claim, which has consequences regarding what counts as good evidence for causal reasoning and mindreading in animals.

Let's begin with the empirical case: Povinelli and colleagues hold that their account provides the best explanation for a wide range of empirical results' (Penn et al. 2008; Gallagher & Povinelli 2012). They survey the psychological literature for abilities that plausibly require reasoning about unobservable variables (e.g., analogical reasoning, transitive inference, causal reasoning, and mindreading).[6] They then argue that the differences between humans and animals on tasks across these domains are best attributed to humans' ability to reason about higher-order relations and animals' failure to do so. Indeed, they believe this difference is stark and widespread. In other words, the hypothesis that reasoning about unobservables requires higher-order reasoning coupled with the claim that only humans are capable of higher-order reasoning is a powerful explanation for a wide range of empirical results regarding the differences between humans and other animals.[7]

One response to this empirical claim is to deny that there is indeed strong empirical support that humans and animals behave differently in the relevant domains (i.e., those domains that are purported indicators of higher-order reasoning). First, Povinelli and colleagues' interpretation of the empirical literature on animals is controversial. Many researchers dispute that there are clear discontinuities between human and animal performance in the relevant domains. For example, comparative cognition researchers Emery & Clayton (2008) argue that Povinelli and colleagues' interpretation of the empirical literature on corvids includes a "number of misinterpretations, absences, and

---

[6] In psychology, analogical reasoning is the capacity to make inferences about a target domain based on analogy to a source domain – if the target and source are similar in some respects, one reasons that they will be similar in other respects. Transitive inference is the ability to deduce a relation between two items based on the known relations between other items (e.g., deducing that x is smaller than z based on the knowledge that x is smaller than y and y is smaller than z). For the sake of argument, I will grant here that these abilities involve reasoning about unobservables, although whether this is the case depends on how one understands the concept "unobservable."

[7] Povinelli and colleagues also present what they call a "representational level" account of why this might be, arguing that humans have a unique "supermodule" that "subserves higher-order, role-governed relational representations in a systematic and domain-general fashion" and that this supermodule "evolved on top of and reinterprets the output of the *proto-symbolic* systems we still share with other animals" (Penn et al. 2008, p. 128). Others have argued that this representational-level account simply redescribes the phenomenon that it purports to explain (Bermúdez 2008, p. 131).

misrepresentations" (p. 135). Also, the emerging consensus in the mindreading literature is that animals such as great apes are capable of various forms of human-like mindreading, such as the attribution of perceptual states (Krupenye & Call 2019). The point here is not which view is correct, but that there is no consensus regarding this empirical claim (see also Lurz et al. 2022).

Povinelli and colleagues might respond that any claims about human-animal continuity in these domains are a product of researchers themselves failing to conduct sound empirical work (Penn & Povinelli 2007; Povinelli and Penn 2011). As noted in Section 2, they argue that although comparative cognition researchers might believe they have positive evidence for some forms of causal reasoning and mindreading in animals because they have successfully rejected various associative-learning alternatives, they have no such evidence. Evidence of this kind instead requires rejecting the alternative hypothesis that animals solved tasks via perceptual abstraction. This response however depends on one accepting Povinelli and colleagues' higher-order reasoning account (as the best account of reasoning about unobservable variables) to begin with. That is, it first rejects the mainstream approach in comparative cognition on the assumption that the higher-order reasoning account is true (which would in turn require that researchers reject perceptual abstraction as a salient alternative hypothesis), and then relies on the rejection of this mainstream empirical approach to support the RR hypothesis. If comparative cognition researchers instead believe that mindreading and causal reasoning require some form of perceptual abstraction (rather than higher-order reasoning), then this is not an alternative hypothesis that must be eliminated before concluding that animals reason about mental states or causes.

Turning now to the analytic case: Povinelli and colleagues sometimes argue that reasoning about unobservables requires higher-order reasoning by definition. For example, in the context of discussing unobservable causal mechanisms, Penn and Povinelli (2007) write: "By 'unobservable' we mean that these causal mechanisms are based on the structural or functional relations between objects rather than on perceptually based exemplars" (Penn & Povinelli 2007, p. 107).[8] However, as we saw in Section 2, higher-order reasoning is also defined as the ability to reason about structural or functional relations as opposed to perceptual features. If this is the case, then reasoning about unobservables is higher-order reasoning by definition. More broadly, Povinelli and Henley (2020) write that weight, mass, force, gravity, and mental states are all unobservable in the sense of being "non-perceptually-based categories and

---

[8] Penn et al. (2008) further write that by "unobservable" they mean those variables that are "in principle unobservable (such as gravity and mental states)" not "temporarily absent or hidden in a particular context" (p. 129).

relations" and that higher-order reasoning allows humans to construct such categories (pp. 393–394). Here again we see that if higher-order reasoning is no more than the ability to construct and reason about "non-perceptually-based categories and relations," then this is definitionally equivalent to reasoning about unobservables. In this case, reasoning about unobservables *requires* higher-order reasoning in the sense that the two forms of reasoning are equivalent.

This analytic position is problematic, however. Most importantly, comparative cognition researchers are typically interested in answering the question, "do nonhuman animals reason about unobservable causes and mental states in the way that humans do?" And answering this question requires empirical knowledge of human cognition. Although researchers might have preconceptions regarding what humans do when they engage in causal reasoning and mindreading, one's view should ultimately be informed by empirical work. Conceptually, it might seem plausible that reasoning about unobservables requires reasoning about structural and functional relations independently of perceptual-based categories. However, evidence is required to show that this is the case. Evidence is required, first, because what seems conceptually true may turn out to be empirically false. A recent example of this comes from work on visual perception. Munton (2022) argues that once we take the dynamic nature of vision into account (i.e., the fact that memory and perceptual representations are interwoven), we find that the "apparent truism about visual perception that we can see only what is visible to us" is false (p. 1). Under the dynamic view, visual experience is best understood as extended across a span of time (say, t_1 to t_5) and what one sees at any given moment depends on this temporally extended experience. Thus, if I see a cat, and the cat is momentarily occluded by an object (i.e., the light reflecting off the cat is not reaching my retina), I may still visually experience the cat at this moment, given my temporally extended experience. If we accept the dynamic view of visual perception based on empirical evidence, then this requires that we revise our conceptual or ordinary understanding of vision: "we can be meaningfully said to see invisible objects" (Munton 2022, p. 344). Similarly, what seems true about a human's capacity to represent unobservable variables might turn out to be false as we learn more about what humans actually do when producing and using such representations. Broadly, the idea that there is a clear distinction between analytic truths (true in virtue of their meaning) and synthetic truths (known by experience) was famously rejected by the philosopher of science Quine (1951). Instead, Quine argued, determining whether a claim is justified depends on both theoretical and empirical considerations. Similarly, an account of what counts as reasoning about unobservables should not be understood as conceptually true independent of empirical work.

Empirical work is also required because there is no consensus regarding what constitutes causal reasoning and mindreading in humans. Povinelli and colleagues themselves note that, like other animals, humans readily rely on perceptual abstraction to solve problems in both the physical and social domains. They write that "some/much/most of the time humans undoubtedly solve problems without recourse to these higher-order variables" (Povinelli & Penn 2011, pp. 75–76). In other words, in the human case, representing unobservable variables is not required for solving many physical and social problems, even when those problems themselves involve unobservable variables (Bermúdez 2003). Moreover, empirical studies suggest that adult humans do in fact rely on a variety of rules and heuristics to solve problems like the trap-tube and string-pulling tasks, rather than abstract causal principles. For example, they avoid unlikely traps and use contact as an indicator of physical connection (Silva & Silva 2006; Silva et al. 2008). Thus, insofar as animals rely on such rules or heuristics, they're solving these problems in human-like ways. Finally, there are alternative non-higher-order-reasoning accounts available for how humans engage in causal reasoning and mindreading. For example, Nichols & Stich (2003) advance a hybrid account of mindreading, involving a range of capacities – some innate, some based on associative learning, some based on the capacity to simulate mental states, and others. The particulars of their account are not critical for our discussion here; what is important is that many researchers find their account theoretically and empirically compelling, despite it diverging significantly from accounts like the RR hypothesis. In short, there is no consensus that reasoning about unobservable mental states and causes requires higher-order reasoning in Povinelli and colleagues' sense. In other words, when humans do what psychologists call "reasoning about unobservables," they may not be doing what Povinelli and colleagues call "reasoning about unobservables."

The main lesson that I would like to draw from this discussion is that it is important not to presume that there is one definitive account of mindreading and causal reasoning that must be adopted across the field of comparative cognition. Instead, any plausible account of what is required to reason about unobservable variables will depend on ongoing research on human and nonhuman animal minds and behavior.[9] Moreover, the nature of this target hypothesis affects what counts as evidence in its favor. Insofar as this hypothesis differs across research groups or over time, what counts as supporting evidence (or what researchers are entitled to expect on the assumption that the hypothesis is true) will also

---

[9] See Colaço (2022) for a nice discussion of how definitions of memory are sometimes best understood as *hypotheses*, rather than expressions of what is already known about memory phenomena.

change. This can lead to disagreements and confusion over whether a hypothesis is warranted, particularly among those who characterize the target hypothesis differently (such as those who disagree about what it means to reason about unobservables).

In the next section, I introduce two additional concerns that must be addressed when evaluating evidence on animal minds. In addition to there being disagreement about what counts as the target hypothesis under study, comparative cognition researchers face problems of underdetermination. This point about underdetermination has been made several times in the recent literature (e.g., Starzak & Gray 2021; Dacey 2023; Halina 2022; Taylor et al. 2022). I highlight what I take to be the major challenges that need addressing and, in Section 4, show how researchers could constrain the hypothesis space in ways that help overcome these challenges.

3.2 Problems of Underdetermination

A major challenge facing current approaches in comparative cognition is that hypotheses are regularly underdetermined by behavioral data. I'll focus on two significant sources of such underdetermination here: First, little is known about the phenomenon under investigation (e.g., the cognitive mechanisms involved in causal reasoning), which means researchers must update the target hypothesis as research progresses (Section 3.2.1). Second, the flexible or accommodating nature of alternative hypotheses means they are difficult to reject (Section 3.2.2). These two sources of underdetermination make it difficult to provide warrant for hypotheses like causal reasoning and mind-reading in animals. However, they are not insurmountable. Overcoming these challenges requires introducing additional constraints on the formulation and evaluation of hypotheses. In Section 4, we consider promising sources for such constraints and how they can be combined with existing research strategies.

Before introducing these two sources of underdetermination, it is worth briefly pausing to consider more generally the nature of target hypotheses such as causal reasoning and mindreading. This is important for both under-standing how they are underdetermined by behavioral data and finding fruitful strategies to overcome this underdetermination. Typically, hypotheses in comparative cognition (like the psychological sciences more broadly) are function-ally or computationally specified. As Heyes (2008) writes, empirical studies on animal minds "postulate functional states and processes, i.e. processes defined in terms of what they do within the information-processing system" (p. 261). If one can successfully subdivide a behavioral capacity into component functions and processes, this is explanatory progress. That is, if the posited cognitive functions do not simply redescribe the behavioral capacity to be explained, then we have learned something new (Dennett 1978). One can then continue in this fashion, breaking down systems into sub-systems, and sub-systems into sub-sub -systems, etc. until eventually the functions that are performed are simple enough that they can conceivably be implemented in a physical system (Dennett 1978; Lycan 1981).[10] Under this view, as William Lycan writes, we "identify mental states (as a first step in the direction of structural concreteness) by reference to the roles they play in furthering the goals and strategies of the systems in which they occur or obtain" (1981, p. 27). One might then draw on neuroscience and biology to identify the entities and structural organization needed to perform the proposed component functions. It is worth highlighting that functional explanations can be intricate and complex. For example, we noted the hybrid account of mindreading advanced by Nichols and Stich (2003) above. Figure 5 depicts this account, illustrating how it provides a functional decomposition of mindreading. Again, the details of the account are not critical for our purposes here. What is important is that each functional component of their model is supported by theoretical and empirical evidence with some proposed functions explicitly advanced as more uncertain or speculative than others.

Sometimes researchers also specify representations as part of their model of how a behavioral capacity is achieved.[11] Whereas a functional description specifies what a component or system does, a representational description specifies the information-bearing structures believed to subserve cognitive functions. It is worth noting, however, that the distinction between functional and representational accounts of cognitive capacities is not necessarily clear cut. For example, drawing on Pierce, Ramsey (2007) characterizes representations in functional terms. He writes that "representations are things that are *used in a certain way*" (p. 23, see also Haugeland 1991). Under this view, the claim that chimpanzees rely on map-like representations when engaging in mindreading, for instance, can be understood as a functional claim: map-like representations play a different role in the economy of internal and external states from, say, linguistic representations (see Boyle 2019). For present purposes, we can say

---

[10] This form of functionalism is what Lycan (1981) refers to as "homuncular functionalist theories" and what Nichols and Stitch (2003) describe as a "boxology" (p. 10). Other variations of functionalism include "task analysis" and "functional analysis by internal states" (see Piccinini & Craver 2011). For the present discussion, nothing hinges on the differences between these accounts.

[11] For examples of representational accounts of mindreading, see Herschbach (2012), Boyle (2019), and Lurz et al. (2022).

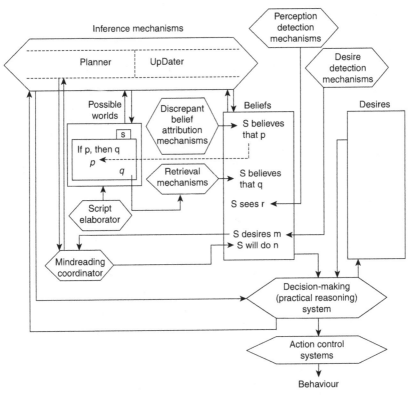

Figure 5 An example of a functional decomposition of mindreading (Nichols & Stich 2003, p. 94). Each component function is advanced based on empirical and theoretical considerations.

that comparative cognition researchers typically generate and test functional and representational hypotheses when investigating animal minds.

3.2.1 Direct Support and Holist Underdetermination

As we have seen, a hypothesis requires direct and indirect support to be warranted. However, such warrant is not obtainable in cases of underdetermination. Broadly, underdetermination is the idea that the available evidence is insufficient to determine whether a hypothesis is warranted (i.e., it is insufficient to decide whether to accept or infer the hypothesis). We have seen cases of underdetermination throughout this Element but let us now spell out two common forms of underdetermination found in comparative cognition.

Holist underdetermination is when the available evidence appears incompatible with one's hypothesis, but it is unclear whether one should reject this hypothesis or some background assumption instead (see Stanford 2023). This form of underdetermination often prevents one from having *direct support* for a hypothesis. When a hypothesis such as, "New Caledonian crows are capable of causal reasoning" is tested, one is not testing this hypothesis in isolation. Instead, researchers rely on many background assumptions, some of which are explicit (e.g., crows can use the tools provided in a trap-tube task) and some of which are implicit. If the results of the test are negative, if crows fail to solve a particular trap-tube task, it is not always clear whether this means that the hypothesis is false (crows lack causal reasoning) or whether some background assumption is false instead (the crows in this task were unable to effectively use the tools provided). Often comparative cognition researchers test their background assumptions to ensure they hold. For example, they will check if study participants can use a tool effectively before providing them with this tool in a trap-tube task. Crucially, however, not all background assumptions can be made explicit or tested in advance. This is particularly the case when there is uncertainty surrounding the target phenomenon under study. Given this uncertainty, researchers are placed in a position of having to frequently update their background assumptions regarding the phenomenon of interest (Boyle 2021; Halina 2021).

In the case of an animal's ability to reason about unobservable variables, we can see background assumptions being regularly updated in the face of conflicting evidence. Consider the case of chimpanzee mindreading research. Early studies indicated that chimpanzees were insensitive to the looking behavior of other agents. For example, they would use a visual gesture (such as an outstretched hand) even when the recipient was not in a position to see this gesture (the recipient's head was turned away, for instance) (Povinelli & Eddy 1996a). Later studies, however, found that great apes do adjust their behaviors in response to where others are looking, leading researchers to explain earlier negative results as a product of false background assumptions (Hare et al. 2000; Kaminski et al. 2004). For example, Brian Hare and colleagues note that earlier studies examined chimpanzees in a cooperative social setting (requesting food from a human provider), rather than a competitive one (stealing food from a competitor). They argue that sophisticated skills like mindreading might emerge only in competitive, rather than cooperative, contexts (Hare et al. 2000). Juliane Kaminski and colleagues additionally argue that the negative results reported by Povinelli and Eddy (1996b) were likely the result of a lack of ecological validity. A study is ecologically valid when its design is consistent with what a participant is likely to experience in a natural setting. Kaminski et al. (2004) note that earlier studies had to train chimpanzees for hundreds of trials to enable them to participate in the study. In contrast, later methods (such as those employed by Kaminski and colleagues) rely on chimpanzees' normal inclination to beg for food. In this case, the background assumption regarding the level of ecological validity required to be a good test for mindreading has been revised. To give a final example, Karin-D'Arcy and Povinelli (2002) failed to replicate the positive results reported by Hare et al. (2000). However, Bräuer et al. (2007) attribute this failed replication to the experimental setting, noting that the distance between food items was smaller in Karin-D'Arcy and Povinelli's study (1.25 m) than in the original study (2 m). They argue that this distance is important because the length of an adult chimpanzee's arm is almost 80 cm. Thus, for such subjects, 1.25 m between food items might not be perceived as a choice. Bräuer et al. (2007) proceed to repeat the original study with a 2 m distance between food items and obtain positive results. In this case, Karin-D'Arcy and colleagues are asked to revise their assumption that a 75 cm difference in distance between food items does not matter.

The above are examples of researchers revising background assumptions regarding the context in which we should expect mindreading to occur in chimpanzees and be detectable by researchers. In the face of negative results, the relevant context is updated or specified more explicitly – researchers decide that social context (competitive versus cooperative) matters, for instance. In addition to these updates regarding context, assumptions about the target phenomenon itself are updated as well. In the case of mindreading, researchers were initially loose in their characterization of nonhuman animal mindreading. For example, Premack and Woodruff (1978) are credited with first asking whether animals have mindreading abilities or "theory of mind." However, in their seminal paper, they do not commit to chimpanzee mindreading taking the exact same form as human mindreading. They write that "we speculate about the possibility that the chimpanzee may have a 'theory of mind,' one not markedly different from our own"; however, they add: "We will not be concerned at this time with whether the chimpanzee's theory is a good or complete one, whether he infers every mental state we infer and does so accurately, that is, makes the inferences on exactly the same occasions we do" (p. 515). Over the next few decades, studies on chimpanzees suggested that they pass some mindreading tasks (those requiring an understanding of other agents' goals, intentions, and perceptual states), but not others (those requiring an understanding of beliefs). This led many researchers to characterize chimpanzee mindreading as different from human mindreading in specific ways. This point is nicely highlighted in a review of thirty years of research on chimpanzee theory of mind by Josep Call and Michael Tomasello. They write:

In a broad construal of the phrase "theory of mind," then, the answer to Premack and Woodruff's pregnant question of 30 years ago is a definite yes, chimpanzees do have a theory of mind. But chimpanzees probably do not understand others in terms of a fully human-like belief–desire psychology in which they appreciate that others have mental representations of the world that drive their actions even when those do not correspond to reality. And so in a more narrow definition of theory of mind as an understanding of false beliefs, the answer to Premack and Woodruff's question might be no, they do not. Why chimpanzees do not seem to understand false beliefs in particular – or if there might be some situations in which they do understand false beliefs – are topics of ongoing research. (2008, p. 191)

Thus, comparative cognition researchers investigate phenomena that are not well defined from the outset or well understood by the research community. Instead, researchers flexibly revise their understanding of a phenomenon (and the context in which it occurs) in response to ongoing research.[12]

One might object that revisions like these should be avoided in scientific research. However, such revisions have been defended as an important feature of general scientific practice (Bechtel 2008; Bechtel & Richardson 2010; Colaço 2020). Focusing on just the comparative cognition case here, we can see that there are several advantages to updating one's understanding of the phenomenon under investigation. First, as we saw above, there is no consensus regarding how best to characterize phenomena such as mindreading and causal reasoning in humans. Research on the cognitive and neural mechanisms under-pinning these phenomena is still in its early stages (Operskalski & Barbey 2017; Wellman 2018), and researchers are only beginning to develop a picture of how these phenomena vary ontogenetically and culturally (Heyes & Frith 2014; Bender et al. 2017; Kulke et al. 2018a). Thus, if the goal is to "clarify the extent to which the cognitive mechanisms possessed by humans are truly shared across taxa" (Krupenye and Call 2019, p. 17), then researchers should expect to revise the target hypothesis in light of ongoing research, given how little we know about how the relevant cognitive mechanisms operate even in the human case. We will return to this point in Section 4.

Second, even if we had a complete and well-evidenced account of phenom-ena such as mindreading and causal reasoning in humans, we would still want to avoid looking for precisely this phenomenon in other animals. To see why, consider recent discussions about this in the context of animal consciousness.

---

[12] A similar dynamic is found in causal reasoning research. For example, Seed et al. (2011) draw on empirical work to inform and revise researchers' understanding of causal reasoning in animals. Specifically, they argue that empirical results suggest one should understand causal properties as falling into perceptual, structural, and symbolic categories (see Seed et al. 2011, pp. 103–107, for discussion).

Birch (2022) describes a "theory-heavy" approach to animal consciousness as taking "a well-confirmed, complete theory of consciousness in humans" and using it to determine whether other animals are conscious (p. 2). As Birch (2022) and Shevlin (2021) argue, one major problem with this approach is that it is too conservative. First, it is unlikely that animals will exhibit a particular cognitive and behavioral capacity in precisely the way that humans do. Second, we know that information-processing capacities such as vision can be achieved in different ways. There is currently no reason to think that capacities such as consciousness, mindreading, and causal reasoning cannot also be achieved in different ways. If one takes a theory-heavy approach to animal minds, then, it will likely result in an unacceptable number of false negatives. As Birch (2022) writes, this is "a cognitively demanding sufficient condition that no non-human animal can meet" (p. 138).

Thus, it is a strength of standard approaches that they make room for revising what one takes to be the target phenomenon. However, this practice opens the door to holist underdetermination. Researchers do not know exactly how mindreading will manifest in chimpanzees, how it will vary across contexts, how it will be affected by different developmental histories, whether it is underpinned in part by associative learning mechanisms, etc. This makes it difficult to provide direct support for a hypothesis such as mindreading because researchers are not certain what pattern in the data one is entitled to expect under the supposition that the hypothesis is true. Although knowledge of human behavior can serve as an initial guide regarding what to expect in other animals, many guiding assumptions will need to revised in the face of conflicting data. Insofar as the hypothesis is a moving target, however, direct support for it will be difficult to come by because what counts as direct support will change over time.[13]

3.2.2 Indirect Support and Contrastive Underdetermination

We have seen that holist underdetermination makes it difficult to provide direct support for a hypothesis. Additionally, contrastive underdetermination makes it difficult to provide indirect support for a hypothesis. *Contrastive underdetermination* is when the available evidence fails to indicate whether we should infer a hypothesis over alternative hypotheses. In other words, the evidence is compatible with more than one hypothesis and thus researchers lack empirical

---

[13] We saw in Sections 2.3 and 3.1 that what counts as a salient alternative hypothesis also depends on how one characterizes the target hypothesis. Given this, updating one's target hypothesis (*h*) may also change what counts as indirect evidence for *h*. For purposes of clarity, I set this point aside here.

reasons for choosing one over the other. Cases of contrastive underdetermination are frequently found in animal mindreading and causal reasoning research.

One reason why contrastive underdetermination is common in comparative cognition is because it is relatively easy to devise alternative hypotheses that can accommodate successful performance on experimental tasks. It is easy in the sense that such alternatives are often unconstrained by theory and evidence. For example, recall that Povinelli and colleagues identify perceptual abstraction as a salient alternative hypothesis to mindreading and causal reasoning. As we saw, the hypothesis of perceptual abstraction holds that most organisms are capable of classifying objects together based on their shared observable properties. Note that this is a very unconstrained account of what animals can do in the sense that the observable objects, shared properties, abstract categories, etc. are all left unspecified (any observable object can be plugged into the account, for instance). As Heyes (2015) notes, such accounts are often "limited by imagination rather than evidence" (p. 321). Given this, the perceptual abstraction hypothesis can be applied to numerous situations, including every result found in the animal mindreading and causal reasoning literature. This leads to the question whether there are any experimental designs that could eliminate perceptual abstraction as a salient alternative to mindreading and causal reasoning. Although Povinelli and colleagues have proposed such designs, others have argued that in these cases too one could explain the positive results by appealing to perceptual abstraction (see Andrews 2005; Lurz 2011; Buckner 2014; Halina 2017a).[14]

We can see now how a hypothesis like perceptual abstraction leads to contrastive underdetermination. An experiment designed to test mindreading and causal reasoning in animals might produce positive results, but insofar as these results can be explained by appealing to perceptual abstraction, one will be unable to choose between these hypotheses based on the empirical results alone. And due to the unconstrained nature of perceptual abstraction, such an alternative will almost always be available.[15]

---

[14] Halina (2015) and Clatterbuck (2018) additionally argue that the perceptual abstraction hypothesis is a version of Carl Hempel's theoretician's dilemma or the idea that any regularity involving theoretical terms can be replaced with a regularity that accounts for the same observable pattern but with the theoretical terms removed (see also Andrews 2017). Applied to perceptual abstraction, one might predict that chimpanzees will categorize perceptual states x, y, and z together due to some theoretical concept they possess (such as a concept of gravity), but if they do indeed reliably categorize these states together, then one could always reinterpret this result not as a product of the chimpanzee's theory or abstract concept, but of some perceptual regularity instead. If this is the case, then perceptual abstraction will always be available as an alternative in mindreading and causal reasoning research, no matter how innovative the experimental design.

[15] Philosophers of science distinguish between transient and permanent underdetermination. Transient underdetermination occurs when the choice between hypotheses is underdetermined

A similar problem arises in mainstream comparative cognition. As introduced in Sections 2.1 and 2.2, the most frequently advanced alternative hypothesis in this context is associative learning, where associative learning accounts hold that most organisms use basic learning abilities to acquire knowledge about relationships between objects and events in their environment. Associative learning is grounded in a long history of empirical work. Researchers have studied phenomena like operant conditioning for over a century (see Thorndike 1911) and have found such learning abilities in a wide range of organisms, from pond snails to humans (Brembs 2003). This explains in part why comparative cognition researchers work hard to eliminate associative learning as an alternative. Nevertheless, associative learning and Povinelli's account of perceptual abstraction share the feature of being able to accommodate an incredibly wide range of empirical results (Buckner 2011; Dacey 2016; Halina 2022). The main reason for this is that the term "associative learning" is used not just to refer to canonical cases of operant and classical conditioning but more broadly to any model built according to associative principles (Buckner 2011). Moreover, what counts as an associative principle has changed and diversified over time (Hanus 2016). These developments are such that it is no longer clear whether it's possible to reject associative learning as a salient alternative explanation in mindreading and causal reasoning research. Even if one were to reject an associative learning explanation for a particular experimental result, this need not prevent one from generating new ones. As Starzak and Gray (2021) write, "associative hypotheses can be constructed *post-hoc* for every experimental outcome" (p. 4). This has led some to conclude that comparative cognition faces an "existential threat" where it is possible to explain *all* behavior by appealing to associative learning (Bucker 2011). Thus, we are faced with another case of contrastive underdetermination: more than one hypothesis can account for the experimental data, preventing researchers from obtaining indirect support for mindreading or causal reasoning in animals.

One might object that the fact that perceptual abstraction and associative learning can account for so many results suggests that there is something wrong with these hypotheses. They are *too* accommodating and thus should be treated

---

by the evidence that we currently happen to have. The expectation here is that collecting more data will allow us to eventually choose between hypotheses. Permanent underdetermination occurs when no amount of empirical evidence will allow researchers to choose between hypotheses. Most cases of underdetermination in comparative cognition are best understood as transient because the underdetermined hypotheses are not expected to have the same empirical consequences across all possible situations. However, perceptual abstraction at times appears to give rise to permanent underdetermination insofar as it is impossible to design experiments that could choose between this hypothesis and others.

with suspicion. Fletcher and Carruthers (2013), for example, argue that perceptual abstraction is "too underspecified to make determinate predictions, hence there is no risk of it turning out to be wrong" (p. 2). This worry is consistent with work in philosophy of science. For example, Douglas (2009) and Douglas and Magnus (2013) argue that novel prediction provides more epistemic warrant than accommodation (where accommodation means that one's hypothesis fits the known data, rather than predicting any new or unknown data). In the case of accommodation, the event or pattern in the data is known; thus, it may have played a role in the construction of the model or hypothesis in question (whether intentionally or not). On the other hand, if a hypothesis makes a novel prediction regarding the relationship between an independent and dependent variable, and this relationship is subsequently found to obtain, then this provides additional assurance that this is a productive way to think about the world (Douglas 2009; Douglas & Magnus 2013). The more a hypothesis can accommodate new data, the greater the concern that it is overfitting the data. Overfitting means that a hypothesis or model fits all the data in a set and thus fails to distinguish between relevant data (data that captures the phenomenon of interest) versus noise or error. Such overfitting means the hypothesis will likely fail to provide new insight into the workings of the world beyond simply capturing the collected data. Perceptual abstraction and associative learning are both shaped by known data in the sense that they are used to explain data that has already been collected by researchers. In the context of mindreading and causal reasoning research, these accounts are not used to make novel predictions. Thus, one might argue that they should be rejected on these grounds, which would solve the problem of contrastive underdetermination.

I agree that prediction provides epistemic assurance above and beyond the accommodation of known results. However, this epistemic advantage alone is not sufficient in my view to remove alternative hypotheses such as associative learning from consideration entirely. The reason echoes what we learned from the case of Clever Hans in Section 2. In that case, researchers found it challenging to discover the cluster of abilities Clever Hans used to select correct answers to mathematical problems. Discovering this required a detailed analysis of the contexts in which Hans was being tested and Hans' behavior in those contexts. Moreover, the cluster of abilities used by Hans was a discovery. It was not known in advance that he could rely on subtle postural cues in noisy settings in this way. Nevertheless, researchers found this explanation of Hans' behavior plausible, given their background knowledge. They thus tested it and found that Hans' responses indeed tracked postural cues, rather than correct answers to mathematical questions.

Similarly, comparative cognition researchers know that most animals rely on attention, perception, memory, associative learning, and other cognitive abilities in their everyday lives. Exactly how these abilities manifest in a particular organism in a particular context, however, is typically not known. Biases acquired over the course of evolution and development affect learning abilities (Cummins 2003; Ginsburg & Jablonka 2019), making it difficult to predict in advance what an organism is capable of learning, how quickly, and how long learned information will be retained. More broadly, neural circuits are continuously resculpted in response to experience (Sterling & Laughlin 2015). Finally, animals often combine abilities in novel and unexpected ways when faced with a new problem and the incentive of a reward. All of this means that when animals solve a task, it is possible they are using a strategy not yet conceived by researchers, despite the strategy being theoretically and empirically plausible, given our background knowledge. Thus, when researchers advance an associative learning alternative to account for an animal's successful performance on a task, such an account may be plausible, given our background knowledge, even in those cases when it was constructed for the sole purpose of explaining the known results of a particular study. In such cases of theoretical and empirical plausibility, researchers are right to treat the hypothesis as a salient alternative that must be eliminated before inferring that the target hypothesis is warranted.

Is it possible to overcome the above problems of underdetermination and, if so, how? In the next section, I argue that an important step in the right direction involves adding new constraints to the construction and evaluation of hypotheses. These purposed constraints should help delimit the behavioral phenomenon of interest, the underlying cognitive mechanisms responsible for that phenomenon, and what counts as a salient alternative hypothesis.

4 Animal Minds: Additional Constraints on Hypothesis Evaluation

Problems of underdetermination are not unique to comparative cognition research but found across the sciences from theoretical physics to molecular genetics (Stanford 2023). One can revise background assumptions in the face of conflicting data and generate empirically equivalent hypotheses across the sciences. Comparative cognition researchers are thus not alone in having to grapple with these problems. The field is relatively unique, however, in that existing methods seem insufficient to manage underdetermination to the degree necessary to obtain strong or moderate support for hypotheses such as mindreading and causal reasoning (see Table 1). Moreover, a consensus regarding the best approach forward does not seem forthcoming. That said, there have been several recent proposals in the literature regarding how to combat these problems. In this section, I build on these proposals. First, I argue that it is important for comparative cognition researchers to draw on a greater diversity of evidence – particularly evidence that gives additional insight into the mechanisms responsible for behavior. Second, I emphasize that researchers will need to revise their accounts of phenomena such as mindreading and causal reasoning in light of ongoing research. This should not be viewed as a barrier to scientific progress, however. Instead, we need an account of progress that reflects this aspect of research practice.

4.1 Signature Testing

There have been several recent proposals in the literature calling for more fine-grained approaches to understanding animal cognition and behavior (Starzek & Gray 2021; Brown 2022; Taylor et al. 2022). The approach advanced by Alex Taylor and colleagues is of particular interest here, as it is advanced with the explicit aim of helping researchers choose among competing hypotheses. Taylor and colleagues refer to mainstream approaches in comparative cognition (such as those introduced in Sections 2.1 and 2.2) as "success testing." Success testing takes place when researchers identify a particular experimental task as a "gold standard" for some cognitive ability (Taylor et al. 2022, p. 738). Successful performance on such a task is then taken as evidence that an animal has that ability. The false-belief task, for example, has been taken by some researchers as a gold-standard test for mindreading.[16]

We have already seen that performing successfully on a particular experimental task is insufficient for inferring that animals mindread. One must eliminate salient alternative hypotheses as well. Taylor and colleagues similarly argue that success testing fails to constrain the hypothesis space sufficiently to determine the cognitive mechanism responsible for successful performance. The solution, they argue, is that researchers should replace success testing with "signature testing." A signature-testing approach is one that identifies the "full

---

[16] Although I agree with Taylor et al. (2022) that some tasks (such as the false-belief task) are sometimes advanced as gold-standard tests for certain cognitive abilities, I think most comparative cognition researchers look at a broader pattern of evidence across many tasks as a good indicator of capacities like mindreading and causal reasoning. Under the latter view, passing a false-belief task while failing other mindreading tasks would be taken as an anomalous result that requires further investigation. Given my disagreement with Taylor and colleagues on this point (i.e., that comparative cognition researchers rely on "one 'gold-standard' problem" (p. 738)), I proceed in this section to use the term "success testing" for the practice of relying on *one or more* pass/fail problem-solving tasks to evaluate the cognitive abilities of animals.

range of information processing patterns including errors, limits, and biases" exhibited by an agent (p. 739). The general idea is that if two species (such as humans and chimpanzees) successfully solve a task (such as the false-belief task), then this only weakly constrains the many hypotheses that can be used to explain this shared performance. However, if humans and chimpanzees are found to exhibit the same pattern of errors, limits, and biases in contexts involving mindreading, then this would provide greater assurance that the same cognitive mechanisms are responsible for the behavior observed in the two species.

Signature testing is already applied in other areas of cognitive science. Consider work on numerical cognition. Humans exhibit a wide range of biases when reasoning about numbers. For example, when asked to bisect a line (mark the perceived center), people exhibit "pseudoneglect" or the tendency to shift spatial attention to the left. Similarly, when asked to "bisect" numbers (estimating the midpoint between two numbers), there is a bias toward smaller numbers. Indeed, those individually who show greater pseudoneglect on spatial tasks exhibit a more pronounced bias toward smaller numbers (Longo & Lourenco 2007). People also associate small numbers with left space and large numbers with right space. For instance, eye moments to the left are initiated faster by small numbers and eye movements to the right are initiated faster by large numbers (Fischer et al. 2004). Eye movements can even be used to predict what number a human participant will randomly generate before he or she verbalizes it: leftward shifts in eye position indicate that the number generated will be smaller than the previous one, and rightward shifts indicate that the number generated will be larger than the previous one (Loetscher et al. 2010). Researchers have taken findings such as these to indicate that numerical cognition in humans relies on a mental number line with numbers increasing from left to right. Finding a similar set of biases in the numerical cognition of other animals would thus provide evidence for a similar underlying cognitive process (see Rugani et al. 2015; Taylor et al. 2022, p. 745).

In my view, one key advantage of signature testing over success testing is that it provides additional insight into *how* an organism processes information (e.g., by mentally representing a number line). A cognitive mechanism can exhibit any number of errors, limits, and biases – thus, the fact that it exhibits one particular cluster of biases, say, over another tells us something about the mechanism's structure. By way of analogy, knowing that birds, bats, and airplanes succeed in flight provides little insight into the mechanisms responsible for their flight. However, if we add information on limits, such as the fact that repetitive flapping in birds reduces their aerodynamic efficiency, whereas this is not the case for bats, then this tells us something about the nature of the underlying mechanisms – in this case, that birds rely on material that wears out (feathers), whereas bats do not (Hedenström et al. 2009). Knowing that an animal succeeds on a task or set of tasks provides some insight into how it achieves this (a certain kind of rigidity in structure is required for flight). However, there is no reason to limit ourselves to knowledge of such successes. Knowledge of errors, limits, and biases provides crucial additional information on how such successes are achieved.

I think signature testing is a major step in the right direction for overcoming problems of underdetermination. However, it should be used in combination with other principles. We saw that alternative hypotheses such as perceptual abstraction and associative learning can almost always (if not always) account for the results of individual studies (Section 3.2.2). Given this flexibility, it is not clear how a focus on errors, limits, and biases could help. In this case, one would simply apply the strategy used to explain individual success tests to individual signature tests. Thus, in addition to signature testing, we must introduce other constraints. Here it is helpful to build on a point we introduced in the previous section: salient alternative hypotheses should be theoretically and empirically grounded.[17] This point is made well by Cecilia Heyes. Focusing on animal mindreading research, Heyes (2015) argues that many alternative hypotheses in this domain lack empirical support. Instead, they include "any conditional statement that a researcher can imagine, referring to behaviour and not to mental states" (p. 321). Heyes argues that researchers should instead take seriously only those alternatives that build on existing work in cognitive science. These hypotheses need not be limited to associative learning but could (and indeed should) draw on any theoretical constructs honed by "careful experimental investigation of robust behavioural and neurological effects" (p. 322). In other words, simply being able to conceive of an alternative account for an experimental result is not sufficient to give it the status of a salient alternative hypothesis. Instead, those advancing such hypotheses must show that they are credible, given our current theoretical and empirical knowledge of animal cognition and behavior.[18]

---

[17] In their proposal for signature testing, Taylor et al. (2022) do not specifically discuss the principle that alternative hypotheses should have evidential support. However, they do highlight the general importance of background knowledge. For example, they write, "background knowledge in any area of science constrains the hypothesis space and, thus, allows us to make useful inferences. Therefore, the diagnostic strength of each signature is determined by the background facts concerning the available hypotheses for how each signature is generated" (p. 746). I take this to be similar to the idea that I'm emphasising here.

[18] As discussed in Section 3.2.2, not every alternative hypothesis will be conceivable in advance of a study. Indeed, some alternative hypotheses might emerge only after the details of an experiment have been analyzed. That is no barrier to the approach advocated here. What is important is that

Signature testing combined with this additional constraint has the capacity to rein in the proliferation of alternative hypotheses. Not only do such hypotheses require theoretical and empirical support, but they must also account for a collection of errors, limits, and biases. Returning to the flight example, one could generate numerous mechanisms that intuitively seem to sustain flight. Only a subset of these will be credible, given our background knowledge (work in aerodynamics, aeroelasticity, etc.). And only a subset of these will be able to account for not only flight, but also the unique suite of errors, limits, and biases found in a particular organism. If we know the rate at which aerodynamic efficiency reduces over time, for example, then this eliminates some wing materials from consideration. Similarly, knowing that an organism can reliably discriminate between large and small quantities of objects provides some constraint on the possible mechanisms responsible for this behavior. However, knowing the specific errors, limits, and biases that an organism exhibits when reasoning about quantities constrains the hypothesis space much further.

There is an additional advantage to moving away from success testing that is worth emphasizing here. Research in comparative cognition is often anthropocentric (or human-centered) in the sense that it focuses on comparisons with humans. Researchers are, after all, typically asking, "do other animals mindread or reason about causes in the way humans do?" What "humans do" is often determined by drawing on previous empirical studies (see Section 2.2). However, sometimes gaps in our empirical knowledge of what humans do and how they do it are filled with assumptions that seem intuitively true. One might hold, for instance, that human mindreading is best understood as requiring higher-order reasoning because this seems intuitively true when one introspects one's own mindreading abilities (Section 2.3). The problem with filling the gaps in this way is that humans are often simply wrong about their own abilities. There is a large empirical literature showing that people tend to overestimate their abilities (overconfidence), believe their own abilities are better than average (the "better-than-average effect"), and view themselves as less biased than others ("bias blind spot") (see Berthet & de Gardelle 2023). Findings such as these have led Buckner (2013) to identify what he calls "anthropofabulation" (a combination of "anthropocentricism" and "confabulation" where the latter involves filling in gaps with fabrications). In the context of comparative cognition, anthropofabulation is what happens when one has a mistakenly inflated conception of what it means to engage in a human activity

---

the alternative hypothesis being advanced is grounded in work in cognitive science before being considered as a candidate for elimination.

such as mindreading, and then relies on this inflated conception as the standard for identifying this capacity in other animals.

Success testing is particularly vulnerable to anthropofabulation. It is vulnerable because it begins with the idea that humans are successful on tasks due to cognitive capacities such as mindreading and causal reasoning. However, as we have seen, we still know very little about how these capacities work. Thus, we might be assuming that they are more powerful, more sophisticated, more uniform, and used more widely than supported by the existing evidence. Shifting our focus to the errors, limits, and biases that humans exhibit when engaged in social and physical problems could help with this. In this case, we are unlikely to have an intuitive (much less exaggerated) sense of our errors, limits, and biases. Thus, we are less likely to fill in empirical gaps with such intuitions.

4.2 Mechanistic Constraints

Signature testing helps constrain the hypothesis space, allowing us to overcome in part problems with underdetermination. Although this will help comparative cognition research move forward, in this section, I argue that there are additional techniques researchers can and should employ to constrain the hypothesis space further. Specifically, they should build on what we know about the neural and other biological mechanisms giving rise to a behavioral phenomenon of interest.[19]

To see this point, it is helpful to briefly introduce the concepts of mechanisms and mechanistic levels. Broadly, a mechanism for a phenomenon involves "entities and activities organized in such a way that they are responsible for the phenomenon" (Illari & Williamson 2012, p. 123).[20] *Entities* are things such as organisms, the hippocampus (a part of the brain), proteins, and neurotransmitters. Entities engage in *activities* or changes in movement and energy: organisms forage, the hippocampus integrates memories, proteins transport molecules, and neurotransmitters bind to receptors. Activities depend on the properties of entities and the surrounding environment. Neurotransmitters (such as glutamate) can engage in binding in part because their three-dimensional structure matches a receptor (the lock-and-key mechanism of binding). Finally,

---

[19] Frans de Waal and Pier Francesco Ferrari (2010) similarly call for what they call a "bottom-up" perspective on animal cognition. Although the spirits of our proposals are similar, our approaches diverge in several respects. For example, de Waal and Ferrari (2010) are not attempting to address problems of underdetermination in comparative cognition, but rather more broadly trying to orient the field away from questions such as "which species can do X?" and towards questions such as "how does X actually work?" (p. 201).

[20] For additional overviews of mechanisms and mechanistic explanations, see Machamer et al. (2000), Bechtel (2008), and Halina (2017b).

mechanisms have *levels* in the sense that an acting entity is itself composed of mechanisms (Craver 2002, 2007). For example, if the acting entity is a foraging organism, then this organism is composed of mechanisms such as those found in the hippocampus allowing the organism to remember the location of fruiting trees. Acting entities on this lower mechanistic level (the hippocampus) are further composed of mechanisms (such as changing patterns of signal transmission between neurons) which are further composed of mechanisms (such as the molecular interactions responsible for signal transmissions between neurons) (Figure 6).

In the context of cognitive neuroscience different research techniques are used to investigate different mechanistic levels. For example, if the acting entity is a behaving organism (what we might call the *organismal level*), then success testing and signature testing (as introduced above) are well designed for investigating such an entity. Such methods are designed to systematically characterize how an organism behaves across a variety of situations. However, if we are interested in the mechanisms responsible for this organismal behavior, it helps to move our investigation down a level to neural systems and their computational properties (what we might broadly call the *neural level*).[21] The techniques used to investigate entities and activities on this level include brain stimulation, brain lesioning, electroencephalography (EEG), positron emission tomography (PET), magnetic resonance imaging (MRI), and others.[22] Broadly, these methods are designed to reveal the entities and activities comprising a neural system, including their properties and organization (e.g., their spatial and temporal features) (see Bechtel forthcoming). For example, by the 1970s, researchers knew that rats with lesions in their hippocampus exhibited deficits in spatial navigation, suggesting that the neural systems responsible for this behavior might be found in this part of the brain. This led researchers to record

---

[21] In cognitive science, the brain and nervous system are typically taken to be proximately responsible for the behavior of an organism. However, often nonneural systems are implicated as well (hormones such as cortisol are linked to cognitive functions like processing speed, but are found in the blood, for instance). Embodied cognition is the view that cognition is a product of both neural and nonneural processes (see Foglia & Wilson 2013; Gallagher 2023). For simplicity, in what follows, I'll use the term "neural mechanisms" to refer to those biological processes responsible for mindreading and causal reasoning behaviors. However, by using this term, I do not mean to exclude the possibility that such capacities depend on nonneural processes as well.

[22] Brain stimulation involves stimulating parts of the brain (e.g., through the implantation of electrodes in the brain) and observing the effects on organismal behavior, while brain lesioning involves measuring the effects on behavior of a part of the brain being diminished or destroyed. Electroencephalography is generally a noninvasive technique that requires placing electrodes on the scalp of an organism and measuring brain electrical activity. Positron emission tomography scans use a radioactive substance (a tracer) to track higher levels of biochemical activity (which in turn may reflect brain activity). Finally, MRI uses strong magnetic fields and radio waves to generate images of brain tissue by monitoring the interaction of protons in the body with magnetic fields.

the activity of individual neurons in the hippocampus. They found that some neurons (dubbed "place cells") fired primarily when an organism was in a particular area of its local environment, suggesting that this population of neurons formed a spatial map of the environment (Bechtel 2016a). Thus, measuring the activity (or lack of activity) of neural systems or populations of neurons can provide insight into the mechanisms responsible for a behavioral phenomenon like spatial navigation.

Mechanisms on the neural level can be further decomposed into entities and activities found on a *molecular level*.[23] The techniques used to investigate mechanisms on this level include gene sequencing (identifying the nucleotides or organic molecules comprising a segment of DNA), gene knockouts

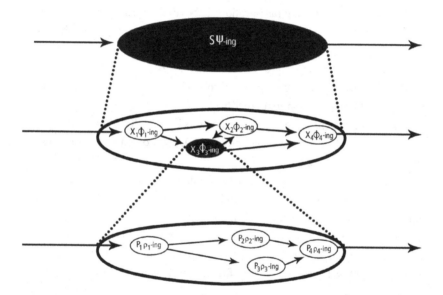

Figure 6 Levels of mechanisms (Craver 2007, p. 189). S ψ-ing (S engaging in activity ψ) represents the phenomenon of interest (top). This phenomenon can be explained by reference to entities (circles) and activities (arrows) organized such that they produce the phenomenon of interest. Each acting entity on this lower mechanistic level (e.g., X_3 ϕ_3-ing) can in turn be explained in terms of a mechanism composed of entities and activities (bottom). Note: ψ-ing is pronounced "psi-ing", ϕ-ing is pronounced "phi-ing," and ρ-ing is pronounced "rho-ing."

---

[23] My aim here is not to provide in any sense a full account of levels of mechanisms in cognitive neuroscience (see Craver (2007) for a more nuanced discussion on this point). Rather, my aim is to illustrate how some research techniques are better suited than others for discovering mechanisms on a particular mechanistic level.

(removing or inactivating genes to prevent their expression), biochemical assays (detecting and monitoring the activities of a range of biological molecules, such as enzymes) and other molecular and biochemical techniques. For example, to better understand the mechanisms underlying 24-hour sleep-wake cycles (circadian rhythms), researchers in the 1970s applied a chemical compound to generate mutations in the X chromosomes of fruit flies (*Drosophila melanogaster*). They found that some of these flies had altered circadian rhythms (e.g., shortened to 19 hours or lengthened to 28 hours). Moreover, these mutations could all be traced to the same gene, suggesting that it played a critical role in the mechanism underlying this behavioral phenomenon. Researchers named the gene *period* and later showed that the expression of this gene resulted in the production of a protein (named PERIOD) that oscillated in concentration every 24 hours (Bechtel 2009).

Comparative cognition researchers follow the discipline of psychology in focusing almost exclusively on the behavior of organisms for constructing and evaluating hypotheses. Both success testing and signature testing focus on the organismal level: success testing collects data on whether agents succeed or fail on problem-solving tasks, while signature testing collects data on errors, limits, and biases exhibited by agents (e.g., where an individual looks before generating a random number). However, it is also widely agreed that a central aim in comparative cognition is to understand the cognitive mechanisms *underlying* behavior. To give a few examples of this sentiment: Schnell et al. (2021a) write, "the field of comparative cognition centres on designing methods to pinpoint the underlying mechanisms that drive behaviors" (p. 162). Gopnik (2013) notes that future work on causal reasoning should address the questions: "What are the actual algorithms used in causal learning? How are they implemented in the brain?" (p. 31). Similarly, Seed and colleagues (2011) ask regarding causal reasoning abilities in animals, "how are they algorithmically and physically realized?" (p. 29). In the context of mindreading, Krupenye and Call (2019) write that cross-species comparisons "require controlled experiments to determine whether superficially similar abilities are actually underpinned by common neural and psychological mechanisms" (p. 16). Thus, researchers aim to discover the cognitive mechanisms underlying behaviors and these mechanisms are typically understood as instantiated in neural processes. Given this, one might ask, "could knowledge of neural processes help constrain the space of cognitive hypotheses examined by comparative cognition researchers?"

Reasons for thinking the answer to this question is "yes" are found in the philosophy of cognitive science literature. For example, Gualtiero Piccinni & Craver (2011) argue that the functional analyses found in psychology are best understood as sketches of neural mechanisms. A mechanism sketch is an elliptical or incomplete account of a mechanism. It leaves out details regarding how the mechanism works. Sometimes these details are omitted intentionally to facilitate communication and understanding, and sometimes they are omitted because they are unknown. In either case, under this view, when a comparative cognition researcher advances a functionally or computationally specified hypothesis (as discussed in Section 3), they are advancing a sketch of a neural mechanism. Understood this way, the fields of comparative cognition and neuroscience are not independent: they aim to describe the same things (neural mechanisms). For any given neural mechanism, researchers from these two fields may emphasize different aspects, but their descriptions should constrain each other. For example, structural components support some functions and not others. As Piccinini and Craver (2011) write, it is "an empirical matter whether the brain has structural components that satisfy a given informational description, that is, whether the neuronal structures in question can sustain the information processing that the model posits (under ecologically and physiologically relevant conditions)" (p. 296). If there is no evidence that the structures required for a given function are present in an organism, then this may lead researchers to reject or revise the functional hypothesis under consideration (see also Boone & Piccinini 2016a).

A similar argument has been advanced in the context of philosophy of biology. Like psychologists, biologists rely on computationally specified hypotheses to explain behavior (Bechtel 2008; Huebner & Schulkin 2022). For example, as suggested above, a major research program in biology and neuroscience is devoted to understanding the behavioral phenomenon of sleep-wake cycles or circadian rhythms. The mechanisms responsible for these sleep-wake cycles in mammals are found in the suprachiasmatic nucleus, a small region of the hypothalamus. Circadian rhythms research, however, differs from comparative cognition research in a striking way. In the former case, researchers aim to empirically discover the parts and component operations posited by a computational model (Bechtel & Abrahamsen 2010). In other words, they seek evidence that allows them to identify the parts (e.g., macromolecules like proteins) and component operations (e.g., the transportation of proteins from the cytoplasm to the nucleus) responsible for circadian rhythms in an organism. Crucially, these parts and operations are not inferred from the behavior of agents alone (i.e., the organismal level). Instead, molecular and biochemical techniques are used to intervene on and observe the entities and activities responsible for circadian cycles (as illustrated above). Computational modeling is then employed to understand how these parts and operations might function to produce the dynamic phenomenon of interest (Bechtel 2016b).

In contrast, as we have seen, comparative cognition researchers follow traditional psychological methods in positing component parts and operations based on the behavior of agents alone. Bechtel and Abrahamsen (2010) argue that such an approach provides weak empirical constraints on cognitive hypotheses (echoing our points regarding underdetermination above). Instead, they argue that circadian rhythms research should serve as an exemplar for work in psychology. Psychologists should anchor their computational accounts in evidence of biological and neural mechanisms.

The idea that identifying the parts and operations of a mechanism is crucial for explanatory progress is highlighted by other philosophers and historians of science as well. For example, Raphael Scholl and Rose Novick argue that such work has been central to overcoming problems of underdetermination in biology. Scholl (2020) argues that the *"vera causa* ideal" has long been a dominant standard of evidence in the life sciences (where *vera causa* is Latin for "true cause"). The *vera causa* ideal holds that one should provide independent evidence that a purported cause exists (the existence requirement). This is in addition to evidence that the cause is responsible for the phenomenon of interest (the competence requirement) (Novick & Scholl 2020; Scholl 2020). According to Scholl and Novick, in the case of biology, the *vera causa* ideal has proved advantageous compared to other evidential standards, such as focusing only on testing the empirical consequences of a hypothesis. They argue that standards like the latter are too liberal. There are simply too many empirically equivalent hypotheses available (i.e., hypotheses with the same empirical consequences). Instead, one should employ the *vera causa* ideal and establish the entities posited by a hypothesis independently (namely, using techniques that target this mechanistic level). The better researchers are at independently establishing the existence of the entities and activities invoked in an explanation (e.g., through improvements in tissue imaging or biochemical assaying techniques), the more closely they approximate the *vera causa* ideal, and the more justified they are in their explanations (Novick & Scholl 2020).

The above accounts converge on the same lesson: the ability to account for an agent's behavior by appealing to a hypothetical or "how possibly" mechanism is on its own weak evidence for the existence of that mechanism. There are simply too many possible mechanisms that can account for data gathered on the organismal level. Given this, many neuroscientists and biologists instead seek to independently identify the parts, operations, and organization of the mechanisms responsible for behavior. They do this by employing techniques designed to manipulate and observe component parts and operations on neural and molecular levels. As we have seen, comparative cognition researchers draw on a wide range of background knowledge when formulating the possible mechanisms responsible for a behavioral phenomenon. Nevertheless, the possibility space remains vast. Cognitive organisms are such that their organismal level behavior alone provides little constraint on determining what is going on in their brains and bodies. Insofar as comparative cognition researchers seek to understand the cognitive mechanisms underlying behavior (rather than simply characterizing behaviors), they should draw on biology and neuroscience to constrain their accounts.

Following Piccinini and Craver (2011), we can understand functional mechanisms like that depicted in Figure 5 as sketching the activities that emerge when neural mechanisms are at work. Indeed, although Nichols and Stich (2003) offer a functional account of mindreading, they do so while recognizing that their explanation will have to be revised in light of neurobiological considerations: "findings about the structure and functioning of the brain can, and ultimately will, impose strong constraints on theories of mindreading of the sort we will be offering" (p. 11). My claim is that comparative cognition researchers should actively seek out such constraints. Although examining errors, limits, and biases as advocated by the signature testing approach will help eliminate some cognitive hypotheses from consideration, constraints from knowledge of neural mechanisms will provide researchers studying animal minds with much needed additional grounding. This grounding is particularly valuable in a field that aims to compare cognitive capacities across a wide range of taxa. When looking at a diversity of species, we can expect some behaviors to look the same, while being underpinned by different neural or biological mechanisms. This is because evolutionary pressures sometimes lead organisms to converge on similar behavioral solutions to ecological problems (e.g., flight as a solution to the problem of locomotion), while the underlying mechanisms giving rise to that behavior differ. In other words, in the same way that the mechanisms underlying flight in birds, bats, and insects differ, the mechanisms underlying causal reasoning in humans and crows may differ, despite behavioral similarities on the organismal level.

This last point can be used to raise an objection to the proposal advanced in this section. One might object that there are numerous ways in which a given psychological state (e.g., a functional specification of mindreading) can be implemented in biological hardware. Such functional accounts would be *multiply realized* in the sense that there would be a one-to-many mapping of functional states to brain states (Putnam 1967). Moreover, the objection goes, it is the role of psychology to construct the best functional account given the behavioral evidence regardless of the fine-grained detail of brain states. It is a separate project to determine how such functional accounts might be implemented in different organisms. The latter project is pursued by neuroscientists and biologists. Psychologists, however, can proceed to construct functional accounts independently of these implementation details. Insofar as comparative cognition researchers follow the methods of psychology, they should similarly proceed independently of knowledge of neural and molecular level mechanisms.

One compelling response to this objection is to simply reject that there is a one-to-many mapping of functional states to brain states in practice. Bechtel and Mundale (1999), for example, argue that proponents of multiple realizability emphasize the commonalities in psychological states across species (e.g., that many species share psychological states such as "seeing") and emphasize the differences in brain processes (e.g., that nervous systems and sense organs often differ in their fine-grained details across species). However, in practice, psychologists have the option of providing more or less detailed accounts of behavior and functions, and neuroscientists have the option of providing more or less detailed accounts of neural mechanisms (Bechtel & Mundale 1999; Bechtel 2008; Cao 2022). Which option they choose depends on the aims of research. In some contexts (e.g., research on individual differences), researchers may differentiate psychological and brain states in a more detailed or fine-grained way. In other contexts (e.g., species comparisons), researchers may differentiate psychological and brain states in a more general or coarse-grained way.[24] If comparative cognition researchers aim to make coarse-grained comparisons across species, they can still do so while drawing on neuroscience to help them choose among competing hypotheses. The relevant neural and biological accounts will in this case be relatively coarse grained. This does not pose a problem, however, because such coarse-grained accounts are commonplace in comparative neuroscience. For example, from a coarse-grained perspective, researchers hold that the neuronal connectivity patterns in the avian pallium (a part of the brain found in birds) are strikingly similar to the connectivity patterns found in the cerebral cortex of mammals. Both have the connectivity of a small-world network with similar modules (e.g., sensory) and functionally analogous hubs (the NCL in birds and prefrontal cortex in mammals) (Shanahan et al. 2013).[25]

---

[24] Applied to flight, one could note that, on a coarse-grained description, the function and structure of flight in birds and bats is the same. Both have rigid structures that enable organisms to remain airborne for some time. However, differences in both structure and function emerge on a fine-grained description: the presence and absence of feathers, for instance, results in different patterns of aerodynamic efficiency, as noted above.

[25] A small-world network is a pattern of connectivity in which most nodes do not neighbor each other, but one can move from one node to another via a small number of steps. See Levy and Bechtel (2013) for a discussion of the importance of small-world organization in the context of abstract mechanistic descriptions.

Of course, there remains a question of exactly how much detail comparative cognition researchers should include in their accounts of animal minds and behavior (whether this detail concerns the organismal, neural, or molecular level). Include too much detail and one fails to identify a cognitive capacity that generalizes beyond a single case. Include too little detail and one fails to capture the phenomenon of interest. All scientific explanations are abstract in the sense that they do not capture everything there is to capture regarding the target of interest (Boone & Piccinini 2016b). Thus, decisions need to be made regarding what to include. It is beyond the scope of this Element to address this issue here. However, any answer will depend in part on what researchers take to be the phenomenon of interest: what is explanatorily relevant depends on what one is trying to explain (see Craver 2007). Thus, let us return briefly to the question of how to identify the phenomenon of interest before concluding this Element.

We saw in Section 3.2.1 that comparative cognition researchers revise the phenomenon of interest based on ongoing research. Researchers have come to view mindreading in chimpanzees, for example, as manifesting more reliably in competitive (rather than cooperative) contexts. This approach toward recharacterizing the phenomenon of interest is found across the sciences. Researchers often observe a target phenomenon across a wide range of controlled situations to determine its precipitating conditions (the conditions sufficient to make the phenomenon occur), inhibiting conditions (the conditions under which the phenomenon fails to occur), modulating conditions (how changes in conditions lead to changes in how the phenomenon occurs), and others (see Craver & Darden 2013, pp. 56–60).

In addition to the above strategy, however, philosophers of science have long highlighted that uncovering the mechanisms responsible for a phenomenon leads to revisions of how that phenomenon is characterized (Bechtel & Richardson 2010; Bechtel 2008; Craver & Darden 2013). For example, mechanism discovery often leads researchers to recognize that they have mischaracterized the phenomenon in the sense of lumping together distinct phenomena or splitting one phenomenon into many (Craver & Darden 2013). For example, consider the case of face recognition discussed by Daniel Burnston and colleagues (Burnston et al. 2011). Researchers in the 1990s hypothesized that an area of the fusiform gyrus (part of the temporal lobe and occipital lobe of the brain) was responsible for human face recognition. Researchers called this area the "fusiform face area" (FFA). Evidence such as the observation that lesions in this area lead to an inability to recognize faces supported this hypothesis. Further research on this brain region, however, indicated that it activated in response to not just faces, but other stimuli as well, such as birds, sculptures, and cars. Moreover, researchers found that activation in this area was higher when a subject was an expert on the stimulus type (e.g., an expert birder or car aficionado). These neural-level discoveries led researchers to revise their understanding of the target phenomenon: it was considered a mistake to split human face recognition from the general phenomenon of categorizing familiar objects. How the phenomenon is characterized in the future will also depend in part on what researchers learn about the mechanisms involved in the FFA and other relevant brain regions.[26]

Thus, how a phenomenon is characterized often "coevolves" with our understanding of its underlying mechanisms (Craver & Darden 2013, p. 62). We may find that mindreading in humans and chimpanzees has similar precipitating, inhibiting, and modulating conditions on the level of the behaving organism. This would be a good initial indicator that mindreading in these two species is underpinned by the same mechanisms. However, an important additional indicator would be the discovery that the neural and/or molecular processes responsible for the behavioral phenomenon of interest are in fact similar. If instead researchers find that the underlying mechanisms are relevantly different, this may lead them to conclude that they have made a lumping error.

The nature of scientific inquiry is such that we should expect a phenomenon to be regularly revised. We should thus not evaluate scientific progress on the assumption that there is a stable or well-established phenomenon already known. Instead, we need an account of scientific progress that recognizes the provisional nature of many behavioral phenomena such as mindreading and causal reasoning. Luckily, such accounts are readily available. Drawing on the history of physics and chemistry, for example, Hasok Chang advances an account of scientific progress in terms of "epistemic iteration" (Chang 2004). Epistemic iteration is a process of self-improvement that occurs through multiple stages of inquiry. It is a process that captures scientific knowledge as something not built on an incontestable foundation, but rather as a process in which "we throw very imperfect ingredients together and manufacture something just a bit less imperfect" (p. 226). Chang shows how temperature research in the eighteenth and nineteenth centuries exhibits iterative progress in terms of enrichment (e.g., precision and scope) and self-correction. For example, with respect to enrichment, measurements of temperature developed iteratively from qualitative assessments (based on human sensations of hot and cold) to ordinal assessments (with the use of thermoscopes) to numerical assessments (with the

---

[26] For additional examples of how mechanism discovery leads to the revision of phenomena, see Bechtel (2008), Bechtel & Richardson (2010), and Craver & Darden (2013). See Colaço (2020) for a discussion on what kind of mechanistic information provides warrant to revise a phenomenon, as opposed to providing a reason to suspend judgment about the phenomenon's characterization.

use of numerical thermometers). With respect to self-correction, Chang shows how later standards for measuring temperature corrected prior standards, despite those later standards being initially based on the prior standards. For example, thermoscopes were used to correct judgments based on human sensation, despite human sensations serving as the original basis for the development and assessment of thermoscopes. Crucially, in cases of epistemic iteration, each stage builds on the previous one, and scientific progress is made despite the fallibility of individual stages. A similar framework can be applied to comparative cognition. Coarse-grained functional accounts can guide research inquiries into underlying mechanisms, while mechanism discovery can lead us to revise our functional accounts in ways that lead to enrichment and self-correction.

To conclude this section, signature testing and knowledge of neural mechanisms provide additional constraints on the cognitive hypothesis space in comparative cognition. I have argued that such constraints are needed to infer hypotheses such as mindreading and causal reasoning in animals. They are needed because organismal-level behavior alone fails to provide sufficient evidence to select among competing hypotheses regarding the mechanisms responsible for behavior. Moving from success testing to signature testing provides a richer account of agent behavior. However, this approach does not seek to directly investigate the component parts and operations of the mechanisms responsible for behavior. Drawing on biology and neuroscience, or those sciences with tools and techniques specially designed to intervene on and observe neural and molecular mechanisms will help provide much needed constraints on the hypothesis space in comparative cognition. Such an interdisciplinary approach also provides constraints on revising the phenomenon of interest, thus helping with problems of holistic underdetermination. Although scientists will always have the option to revise background assumptions in light of conflicting data, having more evidence concerning the entities, activities, and organization of the neural and biological mechanisms responsible for a target phenomenon will provide additional constraints regarding which background assumptions should be revised and why.

Conclusion

The field of comparative cognition aims to better understand animal minds. Although researchers in this field recognize that humans share some cognitive capacities with other animals, they also highlight the diversity of animal minds. Evolution is a process of descent with modification, and animals regularly exhibit unique capacities to adapt to situations through learning and flexible problem solving. The methods of comparative cognition need to be able to handle this diversity. In this Element, we examined the specific question, "Do animals reason about unobservable variables such as causes and mental states?" We have seen that, when addressing this question, comparative cognition researchers face challenges of underdetermination, given the complex, opaque, and clever nature of animal minds.

Researchers work to overcome these challenges by running experiments designed to test target hypotheses (such as mindreading and causal reasoning) and eliminate alternative hypotheses (such as associative learning). These methods help researchers both better understand the target phenomenon, as well as constrain the space of hypotheses that plausibly explain it. Despite these advances, I have argued that additional methods are needed to overcome problems of underdetermination in the field. We have considered two such methods here: signature testing and mechanistic constraints. I have drawn on what we know from work in general philosophy of science and other scientific fields (neuroscience, biology, chemistry) to show how these additional methods can lead to progress in comparative cognition. Although there is much work to be done, comparative cognition is well placed to iteratively improve our understanding of human and nonhuman animal minds.

References

Allen, C. (1992). Mental content. *The British Journal for the Philosophy of Science*, **43**(4), 537–553.

Allen, C., & Bekoff, M. (1997). *Species of Mind: The Philosophy and Biology of Cognitive Ethology*. Cambridge, MA: MIT Press.

Amiez, C., Sallet, J., Novek, J., et al. (2021). Chimpanzee histology and functional brain imaging show that the paracingulate sulcus is not human-specific. *Communications Biology*, **4**, 1–12.

Amodio, P., Boeckle, M., Schnell, A. K. et al. (2019). Grow smart and die young: Why did cephalopods evolve intelligence? *Trends in Ecology & Evolution*, **34**(1), 45–56.

Andrews, K. (2005). Chimpanzee theory of mind: Looking in all the wrong places? *Mind and Language*, **20**(5), 521–536.

Andrews, K. (2012). *Do Apes Read Minds? Toward a New Folk Psychology*. Cambridge, MA: MIT Press.

Andrews, K. (2017). Chimpanzee mind reading: Don't stop believing. *Philosophy Compass*, **12**(1), e12394.

Andrews, K. (2020). *How to Study Animal Minds*. Cambridge: Cambridge University Press.

Arbib, M. A., Liebal, K., & Pika, S. (2008). Primate vocalization, gesture, and the evolution of human language. *Current Anthropology*, **49**(6), 1053–1076.

Baron-Cohen, S., Leslie, A. M., & Frith, U. (1985). Does the autistic child have a "theory of mind"? *Cognition*, **21**(1), 37–46.

Barron, A. B., Halina, M., & Klein, C. (2023). Transitions in cognitive evolution. *Proceedings of the Royal Society B*, **290**(2002), 20230671.

Bausman, W., & Halina, M. (2018). Not null enough: Pseudo-null hypotheses in community ecology and comparative psychology. *Biology & Philosophy*, **33** (3–4), 1–20.

Bechtel, W. (2008). *Mental Mechanisms: Philosophical Perspectives on Cognitive Neuroscience*. New York: Routledge.

Bechtel, W. (2009). Generalization and discovery by assuming conserved mechanisms: Cross-species research on circadian oscillators. *Philosophy of Science*, **76**(5), 762–773.

Bechtel, W. (2016a). Investigating neural representations: The tale of place cells. *Synthese*, **193**, 1287–1321.

Bechtel, W. (2016b). Using computational models to discover and understand mechanisms. *Studies in History and Philosophy of Science Part A*, **56**, 113–121.

Bechtel, W. (forthcoming). The epistemology of evidence in cognitive neuroscience. In R. Skipper Jr., C. Allen, R. A. Ankeny, et al., eds., *Philosophy and the Life Sciences: A Reader*. Cambridge, MA: MIT Press.

Bechtel, W., & Abrahamsen, A. (2010). Dynamic mechanistic explanation: Computational modeling of circadian rhythms as an exemplar for cognitive science. *Studies in History and Philosophy of Science Part A*, **41**(3), 321–333.

Bechtel, W., & Mundale, J. (1999). Multiple realizability revisited: Linking cognitive and neural states. *Philosophy of Science*, **66**(2), 175–207.

Bechtel, W., & Richardson, R. C. (2010). *Discovering Complexity: Decomposition and Localization as Strategies in Scientific Research*. Cambridge, MA: MIT Press.

Bender, A., Beller, S., & Medin, D. L. (2017). Causal Cognition and Culture. In M. R. Waldmann, ed., *The Oxford Handbook of Causal Reasoning*. Oxford: Oxford University Press, pp. 717–738.

Bermúdez, J. L. (2003). The Domain of Folk Psychology. *Royal Institute of Philosophy Supplement*, **53**, 25–48.

Bermúdez, J. L. (2008). The reinterpretation hypothesis: Explanation or redescription? *Behavioral and Brain Sciences*, **31**, 131–132.

Berthet, V., & de Gardelle, V. (2023). The heuristics-and-biases inventory: An open-source tool to explore individual differences in rationality. *Frontiers in Psychology*, **14**, 1–9.

Birch, J. (2022). The search for invertebrate consciousness. *Noûs*, **56**, 133–153.

Blaisdell, A. P., Sawa, K., Leising, K. J., & Waldmann, M. R. (2006). Causal reasoning in rats. *Science*, **311**(5763), 1020–1022.

Boesch, C. (2007). What makes us human (*Homo sapiens*)? The challenge of cognitive cross-species comparison. *Journal of Comparative Psychology*, **121**(3), 227–240.

Boone, W., & Piccinini, G. (2016a). The cognitive neuroscience revolution. *Synthese*, **193**, 1509–1534.

Boone, W., & Piccinini, G. (2016b). Mechanistic abstraction. *Philosophy of Science*, **83**(5), 686–697.

Boyle, A. (2019). Mapping the minds of others. *Review of Philosophy and Psychology*, **10**(4), 747–767.

Boyle, A. (2020). The impure phenomenology of episodic memory. *Mind & Language*, **35**(5), 641–660.

Boyle, A. (2021). Replication, uncertainty and progress in comparative cognition. *Animal Behavior and Cognition*, **8**(2), 296–304.

Bräuer, J., Call, J., & Tomasello, M. (2007). Chimpanzees really know what others can see in a competitive situation. *Animal Cognition*, **10**(4), 439–448.

Brembs, B. (2003). Operant conditioning in invertebrates. *Current Opinion in Neurobiology*, **13**(6), 710–717.

Brown, R. L. (2022). Mapping out the landscape: A multi-dimensional approach to behavioural innovation. *Philosophy of Science*, **89**(5), 1176–1185.

Buckner, C. (2011). Two approaches to the distinction between cognition and "mere association." *International Journal of Comparative Psychology*, **24**(4), 314–348.

Buckner, C. (2013). Morgan's Canon, meet Hume's Dictum: Avoiding anthropofabulation in cross-species comparisons. *Biology & Philosophy*, **28**(5), 853–871.

Buckner, C. (2014). The semantic problem(s) with research on animal mind-reading. *Mind & Language*, **29**(5), 566–589.

Burnston, D., Sheredos, B., & Bechtel, W. (2011). HIT on the psychometric approach. *Psychological Inquiry*, **22**(2), 108–114.

Cao, R. (2022). Multiple realizability and the spirit of functionalism. *Synthese*, **200**(6), 506.

Call, J., & Tomasello, M. (2008). Does the chimpanzee have a theory of mind? 30 years later. *Trends in Cognitive Sciences*, **12**(5), 187–192.

Chang, H. (2004). *Inventing Temperature: Measurement and Scientific Progress*. Oxford: Oxford University Press.

Cheke, L. G., Loissel, E., & Clayton, N. S. (2012). How do children solve Aesop's Fable? *PloS One*, **7**(7), e40574.

Civelek, Z., Call, J., & Seed, A. M. (2020). Inferring unseen causes: Developmental and rvolutionary origins. *Frontiers in Psychology*, **11**, 872.

Clatterbuck, H. (2018). The logical problem and the theoretician's dilemma. *Philosophy and Phenomenological Research*, **97**(2), 322–350.

Claudio, Tennie, C., Völter, C. J., Vonau, V., Hanus, D., Call, J., & Tomasello, M. (2019). Chimpanzees use observed temporal directionality to learn novel causal relations. *Primates*, **60**, 517–524.

Clayton, N. S., & Dickinson, A. (1998). Episodic-like memory during cache recovery by scrub jays. *Nature*, **395**(6699), 272–274.

Clayton, N. S., Griffiths, D. P., Emery, N. J., & Dickinson, A. (2001). Elements of episodic–like memory in animals. *Philosophical Transactions of the Royal Society of London. Series B: Biological Sciences*, **356**(1413), 1483–1491.

Colaço, D. (2020). Recharacterizing scientific phenomena. *European Journal for Philosophy of Science*, **10**(14), 1–19.

Colaço, D. (2022). What counts as a memory? Definitions, hypotheses, and "kinding in progress." *Philosophy of Science*, **89**(1), 89–106.

Craver, C. F. (2002). Interlevel experiments and multilevel mechanisms in the neuroscience of memory. *Philosophy of Science*, **69**(S3), S83–S97.

Craver, C. F. (2007). *Explaining the brain: Mechanisms and the mosaic unity of neuroscience*. Oxford: Oxford University Press.

Craver, C. F., & Darden, L. (2013). *In Search of Mechanisms: Discoveries Across the Life Sciences*. Chicago: University of Chicago Press.

Craver, C. F., Kwan, D., Steindam, C., & Rosenbaum, R. S. (2014). Individuals with episodic amnesia are not stuck in time. *Neuropsychologia*, **57**, 191–195.

Crystal, J. D. (2018). Animal models of episodic memory. *Comparative Cognition & Behavior Reviews*, **13**, 105–122.

Cummins, D. D. (2003). The evolution of reasoning. In J. P. Leighton & R. J. Sternberg, eds., *The Nature of Reasoning*, 1st ed., Cambridge: Cambridge University Press, pp. 339–374.

Currie, A. (2021). *Comparative Thinking in Biology*, 1st ed., Cambridge: Cambridge University Press. http://doi.org/10.1017/9781108616683.

Dacey, M. (2016). Rethinking associations in psychology. *Synthese*, **193**(12), 3763–3786.

Dacey, M. (2023). Evidence in default: Rejecting default models of animal minds. The British Journal for the *Philosophy of Science*, **74**(2), 291–532.

Dalla Barba, G., & La Corte, V. (2013). The hippocampus, a time machine that makes errors. *Trends in Cognitive Sciences*, **17**(3), 102–104.

Darwin, C. (1875). *The Descent of Man, and Selection in Relation to Sex*. New York: D. Appleton.

de Waal, F. B. M., & Ferrari, P. F. (2010). Towards a bottom-up perspective on animal and human cognition. *Trends in Cognitive Sciences*, **14**(5), 201–207.

De Regt, H. W. (2017). *Understanding Scientific Understanding*. Oxford: Oxford University Press.

Dennett, D. C. (1978). *Brainstorms*. Montgomery: Bradford Books.

Devine, R. T., & Hughes, C. (2014). Relations between false belief understanding and executive function in early childhood: A meta-analysis. *Child Development*, **85**(5), 1777–1794.

Douglas, H. E. (2009). Reintroducing prediction to explanation. *Philosophy of Science*, **76**(4), 444–463.

Douglas, H., & Magnus, P. D. (2013). State of the field: Why novel prediction matters. *Studies in History and Philosophy of Science Part A*, **44**(4), 580–589.

Emery, N. J., & Clayton, N. S. (2008). Imaginative scrub-jays, causal rooks, and a liberal application of Occam's aftershave. *Behavioral and Brain Sciences*, **31**, 134–135.

Fischer, M. H., Warlop, N., Hill, R. L., & Fias, W. (2004). Oculomotor bias induced by number perception. *Experimental Psychology*, **51**(2), 91–97.

Fletcher, L., & Carruthers, P. (2013). Behavior-reading versus mentalizing in animals. In J. Metcalfe & H. S. Terrace, eds., *Agency and Joint Attention*. Oxford. Oxford University Press, pp. 82–99.

Foglia, L., & Wilson, R. A. (2013). Embodied cognition. *Wiley Interdisciplinary Reviews: Cognitive Science*, 4(3), 319–325.

Gallagher, S. (2023). *Embodied and Enactive Approaches to Cognition*. Cambridge: Cambridge University Press.

Gallagher, S., & Povinelli, D. J. (2012). Enactive and behavioral abstraction accounts of social understanding in chimpanzees, infants, and adults. *Review of Philosophy and Psychology*, 3, 145–169.

Ginsburg, S., & Jablonka, E. (2019). *The Evolution of The Sensitive Soul: Learning and The Origins of Consciousness*. Cambridge, MA: MIT Press.

Gopnik, A. (2013). Causality. In P. D. Zelazo, ed., *The Oxford Handbook of Developmental Psychology, Vol. 1*. Oxford: Oxford University Press, pp. 627–650.

Halina, M., Rossano, F., & Tomasello, M. (2013). The ontogenetic ritualization of bonobo gestures. *Animal Cognition*, **16**, 653–666.

Halina, M. (2015). There is no special problem of mindreading in nonhuman animals. *Philosophy of Science*, **82**(3), 473–490.

Halina, M. (2017a). What apes know about seeing. In K. Andrews & J. Beck, eds., *The Routledge Handbook of Philosophy of Animal Minds*. New York: Routledge, pp. 238–246.

Halina, M. (2017b). Mechanistic explanation and its limits. In S. Glennan & P. Illari, eds., *The Routledge Handbook of Mechanisms and Mechanical Philosophy*. New York: Routledge, pp. 213–224.

Halina, M. (2021). Replications in comparative psychology. *Animal Behavior and Cognition*, **8**(2), 263–272.

Halina, M. (2022). Unlimited associative learning as a null hypothesis. *Philosophy of Science*, **89**(5), 1186–1195.

Halina, M. (2023). Methods in comparative cognition. In E. N. Zalta & U. Nodelman, eds., *The Stanford Encyclopedia of Philosophy* (Fall 2023 Edition). https://plato.stanford.edu/archives/fall2023/entries/comparative-cognition/.

Halina, M., & Bechtel, W. (2013). Mechanism, conserved. In W. Dubitzky, O. Wolkenhauer, K.-H. Cho, & H. Yokota, eds., *Encyclopedia of Systems Biology*, New York: Springer, pp. 1201–1204.

Hanus, D. (2016). Causal reasoning versus associative learning: A useful dichotomy or a strawman battle in comparative psychology? *Journal of Comparative Psychology*, **130**(3), 241–248.

Hare, B., Call, J., Agnetta, B., & Tomasello, M. (2000). Chimpanzees know what conspecifics do and do not see. *Animal Behaviour*, **59**(4), 771–785.

Haugeland, J. (1991). Representational genera. In W. Ramsey, S. Stich, & D. Rumelhart, eds., *Philosophy and Connectionist Theory*. Hillsdale, NJ: Lawrence Erlbaum, pp. 61–89.

Healy, S., & Braithwaite, V. (2000). Cognitive ecology: A field of substance? *Trends in Ecology & Evolution*, **15**(1), 22–26.

Healy, S. D., & Andrew Hurly, T. (2003). Cognitive ecology: Foraging in hummingbirds as a model system. In P. J. B. Slater, J. S. Rosenblatt, C. T. Snowdon & T. J. Roper, eds., *Advances in the Study of Behavior*. San Diego, CA: Elsevier Science, pp. 325–359.

Healy, S. D., Bacon, I. E., Haggis, O., Harris, A. P., & Kelley, L. A. (2009). Explanations for variation in cognitive ability: Behavioural ecology meets comparative cognition. *Behavioural Processes*, **80**(3), 288–294.

Healy, S. D., & Jones, C. M. (2002). Animal learning and memory: An integration of cognition and ecology. *Zoology*, **105**(4), 321–327.

Hedenström, A., Johansson, L. C., & Spedding, G. R. (2009). Bird or bat: Comparing airframe design and flight performance. *Bioinspiration & Biomimetics*, **4**(1), 1–13.

Herrmann, E., Call, J., Hernandez-Lloreda, M. V., Hare, B., & Tomasello, M. (2007). Humans have evolved specialized skills of social cognition: The cultural intelligence hypothesis. *Science*, **317**(5843), 1360–1366.

Herschbach, M. (2012). Mirroring versus simulation: On the representational function of simulation. *Synthese*, **189**(3), 483–513.

Heyes, C. (2008). Beast machines? Questions of animal consciousness. In L Weiskrantz & M. Davies, eds., *Frontiers of Consciousness: Chichele Lectures*. Oxford: Oxford University Press, pp. 259–274.

Heyes, C. (2014a). False belief in infancy: A fresh look. *Developmental Science*, **17**(5), 647–659.

Heyes, C. (2014b). Submentalizing: I am not really reading your mind. *Perspectives on Psychological Science*, **9**(2), 131–143.

Heyes, C. (2015). Animal mindreading: What's the problem? *Psychonomic Bulletin & Review*, **22**(2), 313–327.

Heyes, C. (2017). Apes submentalise. *Trends in Cognitive Sciences*, **21**(1), 1–2.

Heyes, C. M., & Frith, C. D. (2014). The cultural evolution of mind reading. *Science*, **344**(6190), 1243091.

Howard, S. R., Avarguès-Weber, A., Garcia, J. E., Greentree, A. D., & Dyer, A. G. (2018). Numerical ordering of zero in honey bees. *Science*, **360** (6393), 1124–1126.

Huebner, B., & Schulkin, J. (2022). *Biological Cognition*. Cambridge: Cambridge University Press.

Illari, P. M., & Williamson, J. (2012). What is a mechanism? Thinking about mechanisms across the sciences. *European Journal for Philosophy of Science*, **2**, 119–135.

Jacobs, I. F., & Osvath, M. (2015). The string-pulling paradigm in comparative psychology. *Journal of Comparative Psychology*, **129**(2), 89–120.

Jelbert, S. A., Taylor, A. H., & Gray, R. D. (2015). Investigating animal cognition with the Aesop's Fable paradigm: Current understanding and future directions. *Communicative & Integrative Biology*, **8**(4), e1035846.

Jelbert, S. A., Miller, R., Schiestl, M., Boeckle, M., Cheke, L. G., Gray, R. D. et al. (2019). New Caledonian crows infer the weight of objects from observing their movements in a breeze. *Proceedings of the Royal Society B*, **286**(1894), 20182332.

Jozet-Alves, C., Bertin, M., & Clayton, N. S. (2013). Evidence of episodic-like memory in cuttlefish. *Current Biology*, **23**(23), R1033–R1035.

Karin-D'Arcy, R. M., & Povinelli, D. J. (2002). Do chimpanzees know what each other see? A closer look. *International Journal of Comparative Psychology*, **15**(1), 21–54.

Kaminski, J. (2015). Theory of mind: A primatological perspective. In W. Henke & I. Tattersall, eds., *Handbook of Paleoanthropology*, Berlin: Springer, pp. 1741–1757.

Kaminski, J., Call, J., & Tomasello, M. (2004). Body orientation and face orientation: Two factors controlling apes' begging behavior from humans. *Animal Cognition*, **7**(4), 216–223.

Kampis, D., Kármán, P., Csibra, G., Southgate, V., & Hernik, M. (2021). A two-lab direct replication attempt of Southgate, Senju and Csibra (2007). *Royal Society Open Science*, **8**(8), 210190.

Kano, F., Krupenye, C., Hirata, S., Call, J., & Tomasello, M. (2017). Submentalizing cannot explain belief-based action anticipation in apes. *Trends in Cognitive Sciences*, **21**(9), 633–634.

Krupenye, C., Kano, F., Hirata, S., Call, J., & Tomasello, M. (2016). Great apes anticipate that other individuals will act according to false beliefs. *Science*, **354**(6308), 110–114.

Krupenye, C., Kano, F., Hirata, S., Call, J., & Tomasello, M. (2017). A test of the submentalizing hypothesis: Apes' performance in a false belief task inanimate control. *Communicative & Integrative Biology*, **10**(4), e1343771.

Krupenye, C., & Call, J. (2019). Theory of mind in animals: Current and future directions. *WIREs Cognitive Science*, **10**(6), e1503.

Kulke, L., Reiß, M., Krist, H., & Rakoczy, H. (2018a). How robust are anticipatory looking measures of theory of mind? Replication attempts across the life span. *Cognitive Development*, **46**, 97–111.

Levy, A., & Bechtel, W. (2013). Abstraction and the organization of mechanisms. *Philosophy of Science*, **80**(2), 241–261.

Loetscher, T., Bockisch, C. J., Nicholls, M. E., & Brugger, P. (2010). Eye position predicts what number you have in mind. *Current Biology*, **20**(6), R264–R265.

Longo, M. R., & Lourenco, S. F. (2007). Spatial attention and the mental number line: Evidence for characteristic biases and compression. *Neuropsychologia*, **45**(7), 1400–1407.

Lurz, R. W. (2011). *Mindreading Animals: The Debate Over What Animals Know About Other Minds*. Cambridge, MA: MIT Press.

Lurz, R. W., Krachun, C., Mareno, M. C., & Hopkins, W. D. (2022). Do chimpanzees predict others' behavior by simulating their beliefs? *Animal Behavior and Cognition*, **9**(2), 153–175.

Lycan, W. (1981). Form, function, and feel. *The Journal of Philosophy*, **78**(1), 24–50.

Machamer, P., Darden, L., & Craver, C. F. (2000). Thinking about mechanisms. *Philosophy of Science*, **67**(1), 1–25.

MacLean, E. L., Matthews, L. J., Hare, B. A., et al. (2012). How does cognition evolve? Phylogenetic comparative psychology. *Animal Cognition*, **15**(2), 223–238.

Meketa, I. (2014). A critique of the principle of cognitive simplicity in comparative cognition. *Biology & Philosophy*, **29**(5), 731–745.

Munton, J. (2022). How to see invisible objects. *Noûs*, **56**(2), 343–365.

Nichols, S., & Stich, S. P. (2003). *Mindreading: An Integrated Account of Pretence, Self-awareness, and Understanding Other Minds*. Oxford: Oxford University Press.

Novick, A., & Scholl, R. (2020). Presume it not: True causes in the search for the basis of heredity. *The British Journal for the Philosophy of Science*, **71**(1), 59–86.

Onishi, K. H., & Baillargeon, R. (2005). Do 15-month-old infants understand false beliefs? *Science*, **308**(5719), 255–258.

Operskalski, J. T., & Barbey, A. K. (2017). Cognitive neuroscience of causal reasoning. In M. Waldmann, ed., *The Oxford Handbook of Causal Reasoning*. Oxford: Oxford University Press, pp. 217–242.

Panoz-Brown, D., Iyer, V., Carey, L. M., et al. (2018). Replay of episodic memories in the rat. *Current Biology*, **28**(10), 1628–1634.

Penn, D. C., Holyoak, K. J., & Povinelli, D. J. (2008). Darwin's mistake: Explaining the discontinuity between human and nonhuman minds. *Behavioural and Brain Sciences*, **31**(2), 109–130.

Penn, D. C., & Povinelli, D. J. (2007). On the lack of evidence that non-human animals possess anything remotely resembling a "theory of mind." *Philosophical Transactions of the Royal Society B: Biological Sciences*, **362**(1480), 731–744.

Pfungst, O. (1911/2010). *Clever Hans (the Horse of Mr. Von Osten): A Contribution to Experimental Animal and Human Psychology.* New York: Henry Holt.

Piccinini, G., & Craver, C. (2011). Integrating psychology and neuroscience: Functional analyses as mechanism sketches. *Synthese*, **183**(3), 283–311.

Pika, S., Liebal, K., Call, J., & Tomasello, M. (2007). The gestural communication of apes. In K. Liebal, C. Müller, & S. Pika, eds., *Benjamins Current Topics*. Amsterdam: John Benjamins, pp. 35–49.

Pollick, A. S., & de Waal, F. B. M. (2007). Ape gestures and language evolution. *Proceedings of the National Academy of Sciences*, **104**(19), 8184–8189.

Povinelli, D. J. (2020). Can comparative psychology crack its toughest nut? *Animal Behavior and Cognition*, **7**(4), 589–652.

Povinelli, D. J., & Eddy, T. J. (1996a). Chimpanzees: Joint visual attention. *Psychological Science*, **7**(3), 129–135.

Povinelli, D. J., & Eddy, T. J. (1996b). What young chimpanzees know about seeing. *Monographs of the Society for Research in Child Development*, **61**(3), v–vi, 1–191.

Povinelli, D. J., & Henley, T. (2020). More rope tricks reveal why more task variants will never lead to strong inferences about higher-order causal reasoning in chimpanzees. *Animal Behavior and Cognition*, **7**(3), 392–418.

Povinelli, D. J., & Penn, D. C. (2011). Through a floppy tool darkly. In T. McCormack, C. Hoerl, & S. Butterfill, eds., *Tool Use and Causal Cognition*. Oxford: Oxford University Press, pp. 69–88.

Povinelli, D. J., & Vonk, J. (2004). We don't need a microscope to explore the chimpanzee's mind. *Mind and Language*, **19**(1), 1–28.

Pravosudov, V. V., & Roth II, T. C. (2013). Cognitive ecology of food hoarding: The evolution of spatial memory and the hippocampus. *Annual Review of Ecology, Evolution, and Systematics*, **44**(1), 173–193.

Premack, D., & Woodruff, G. (1978). Does the chimpanzee have a theory of mind? *Behavioral and Brain Sciences*, **1**(4), 515–526.

Putnam, H. (1967). Psychological Predicates. In W. H. Capitan and D. D. Merrill, eds., *Art, Mind, and Religion*. Pittsburgh: University of Pittsburgh Press, pp. 37–48.

Quine, W. V. O. (1951). Two dogmas of empiricism. Reprinted in a *Logical Point of View*, 2nd ed., Cambridge, MA: Harvard University Press, pp. 20–46.

Ramsey, W. M. (2007). *Representation Reconsidered*. Cambridge: Cambridge University Press.

Reiss, J. (2015). A pragmatist theory of evidence. *Philosophy of Science*, **82**(3), 341–362.

Reiss, J. (2019). Against external validity. *Synthese*, **196**(8), 3103–3121.

Rugani, R., Vallortigara, G., Priftis, K., & Regolin, L. (2015). Number-space mapping in the newborn chick resembles humans' mental number line. *Science*, **347**(6221), 534–536.

Schnell, A. K., Amodio, P., Boeckle, M., & Clayton, N. S. (2021a). How intelligent is a cephalopod? Lessons from comparative cognition. *Biological Reviews*, **96**(1), 162–178.

Schnell, A. K., Clayton, N. S., Hanlon, R. T., & Jozet-Alves, C. (2021b). Episodic-like memory is preserved with age in cuttlefish. *Proceedings of the Royal Society B: Biological Sciences*, **288**(1957), 20211052.

Scholl, R. (2020). Unwarranted assumptions: Claude Bernard and the growth of the vera causa standard. *Studies in History and Philosophy of Science Part A*, **82**, 120–130.

Seed, A. M., Tebbich, S., Emery, N. J., & Clayton, N. S. (2006). Investigating physical cognition in rooks, *Corvus frugilegus*. *Current Biology*, **16**(7), 697–701.

Seed, A., Hanus, D., & Call, J. (2011). Causal knowledge in corvids, primates, and children. In T. McCormack, C. Hoerl, & S. Butterfill, eds., *Tool Use and Causal Cognition*. Oxford: Oxford University Press, pp. 89–110.

Shanahan, M., Bingman, V. P., Shimizu, T., Wild, M., & Güntürkün, O. (2013). Large-scale network organization in the avian forebrain: A connectivity matrix and theoretical analysis. *Frontiers in Computational Neuroscience*, **7**(89), 1–17.

Shettleworth, S. J. (2010). Clever animals and killjoy explanations in comparative psychology. *Trends in Cognitive Sciences*, **14**(11), 477–481.

Shettleworth, S. J. (2012). *Fundamentals of Comparative Cognition*. Oxford: Oxford University Press.

Shevlin, H. (2021). Non-human consciousness and the specificity problem: A modest theoretical proposal. *Mind & Language*, **36**(2), 297–314.

Silva, F. J., & Silva, K. M. (2006). Humans' folk physics is not enough to explain variations in their tool-using behavior. *Psychonomic Bulletin & Review*, **13**(4), 689–693.

Silva, F. J., Silva, K. M., Cover, K. R., Leslie, A. L., & Rubalcaba, M. A. (2008). Humans' folk physics is sensitive to physical connection and contact between a tool and reward. *Behavioural Processes*, **77**(3), 327–333.

Sober, E. (2012). Anthropomorphism, parsimony, and common ancestry. *Mind & Language*, **27**(3), 229–238.

Southgate, V., Senju, A., & Csibra, G. (2007). Action anticipation through attribution of false belief by 2-year-olds. *Psychological Science*, **18**(7), 587–592.

Stanford, P. K. (2006). *Exceeding Our Grasp: Science, History, and the Problem of Unconceived Alternatives*. Oxford: Oxford University Press.

Stanford, K. (2023). Underdetermination of scientific theory. In E. N. Zalta & U. Nodelman, eds., *The Stanford Encyclopedia of Philosophy* (Summer 2023 Edition). https://plato.stanford.edu/archives/sum2023/entries/scientific-underdetermination/.

Starzak, T. B., & Gray, R. D. (2021). Towards ending the animal cognition war: A three-dimensional model of causal cognition. *Biology & Philosophy*, **36**(2), 1–24.

Sterelny, K. (2010). Minds: Extended or scaffolded? *Phenomenology and the Cognitive Sciences*, **9**(4), 465–481.

Sterling, P., & Laughlin, S. (2015). *Principles of Neural Design*. Cambridge, MA: MIT Press.

Suddendorf, T., & Busby, J. (2003). Mental time travel in animals? *Trends in Cognitive Sciences*, **7**(9), 391–396.

Surian, L., Caldi, S., & Sperber, D. (2007). Attribution of beliefs by 13-month-old infants. *Psychological Science*, **18**(7), 580–586.

Taylor, A. H. (2020). Folk physics for crows? *Animal Behavior and Cognition*, **7**(3), 452–456.

Taylor, A. H., Bastos, A. P., Brown, R. L., & Allen, C. (2022). The signature-testing approach to mapping biological and artificial intelligences. *Trends in Cognitive Sciences*, **26**(9), 738–750.

Thorndike, E. L. (1911). *Animal Intelligence: Experimental Studies*. New York: The MacMillan.

Tomasello, M., & Call, J. (2008). Assessing the validity of ape-human comparisons: A reply to Boesch (2007). *Journal of Comparative Psychology*, **122**(4), 449–452.

Tomasello, M., & Call, J. (2019). Thirty years of great ape gestures. *Animal Cognition*, **22**(4), 461–469.

Trestman, M. (2015). Clever Hans, Alex the parrot, and Kanzi: What can exceptional animal learning teach us about human cognitive evolution? *Biological Theory*, **10**(1), 86–99.

Veit, L., & Nieder, A. (2013). Abstract rule neurons in the endbrain support intelligent behaviour in corvid songbirds. *Nature Communications*, **4**(1), 2878.

Versace, E., Martinho-Truswell, A., Kacelnik, A., & Vallortigara, G. (2018). Priors in animal and artificial intelligence: Where does learning begin? *Trends in Cognitive Sciences*, **22**(11), 963–965.

Visalberghi, E., & Limongelli, L. (1994). Lack of comprehension of cause-effect relations in tool-using capuchin monkeys (*Cebus apella*). *Journal of Comparative Psychology*, **108**(1), 15–22.

Visalberghi, E., & Tomasello, M. (1998). Primate causal understanding in the physical and psychological domains. *Behavioural Processes*, **42**, 189–203.

Völter, C. J., Sentís, I., & Call, J. (2016). Great apes and children infer causal relations from patterns of variation and covariation. *Cognition*, **155**, 30–43.

von Bayern, A. M. P., Heathcote, R. J. P., Rutz, C., & Kacelnik, A. (2009). The role of experience in problem solving and innovative tool use in crows. *Current Biology*, **19**(22), 1965–1968.

von Bayern, A. M. P., von, Danel, S., Auersperg, A. M. I., Mioduszewska, B., & Kacelnik, A. (2018). Compound tool construction by New Caledonian crows. *Scientific Reports*, **8**(1), 15676.

Vonk, J. (2020). Sticks and stones: Associative learning alone? *Learning & Behavior*, **48**(3), 277–278.

Vonk, J., & Povinelli, D. J. (2012). Similarity and difference in the conceptual systems of primates: The unobservability hypothesis. In T. R. Zentall & E. A. Wasserman, eds., *The Oxford Handbook of Comparative Cognition*. Oxford: Oxford University Press, pp. 552–576.

Wellman, H. M. (2018). Theory of mind: The state of the art. *European Journal of Developmental Psychology*, **15**(6), 728–755.

Acknowledgments

Many thanks to Mike Dacey, Keith Frankish, Scott Partington, and two anonymous reviewers for their valuable feedback on earlier versions of this manuscript. This research was supported in part by a grant from the Templeton World Charity Foundation.

Cambridge Elements ☰

Philosophy of Mind

Keith Frankish

The University of Sheffield

Keith Frankish is a philosopher specializing in philosophy of mind, philosophy of psychology, and philosophy of cognitive science. He is the author of *Mind and Supermind* (Cambridge University Press, 2004) and *Consciousness* (2005), and has also edited or coedited several collections of essays, including *The Cambridge Handbook of Cognitive Science* (Cambridge University Press, 2012), *The Cambridge Handbook of Artificial Intelligence* (Cambridge University Press, 2014) (both with William Ramsey), and *Illusionism as a Theory of Consciousness* (2017).

About the Series

This series provides concise, authoritative introductions to contemporary work in philosophy of mind, written by leading researchers and including both established and emerging topics. It provides an entry point to the primary literature and will be the standard resource for researchers, students, and anyone wanting a firm grounding in this fascinating field.

Cambridge Elements ≡

Philosophy of Mind

Printed in the United States
by Baker & Taylor Publisher Services